ISBN: 978-1-7360852-1-9

#7-FIGURE
NET WORTH

MODERN WEALTH

BLUEPRINT FOR

BLACK AMERICANS

BRIELLE MABREY

Sage Insights Publishing

For my intelligent,
inquisitive, and spirited daughters
as well as future generations
of brown skin babies.

May your financial futures be vibrant!

Contents

Your Mindset

Your Legacy

Thank You!

I have a whole new appreciation for this page giving expressions of gratitude within a book now. This has *genuinely* been the effort of a village and I am incredibly grateful.

First, I want to thank Yahuah (My Father God) for trusting me to steward this message. I am so humbled that You inspired me, nudged me, and were patient with my moments of resistance. I am truly grateful that You led me to and entrusted me with this work.

Next, I have to absolutely thank my phenomenal husband, my rock, my plumbline Nathaniel.

Without you, this would *not* have happened. Thank you for supporting this vision not just philosophically but literally by getting into the trenches with me—as a sounding board, an editor, and a researcher. Thank you for everything you did to keep our home and the girls happy on the countless evenings that I camped out with my laptop at the dining room table.

Sending huge hugs and deep appreciation to my two kind, smart, inquisitive, and spirited daughters. You two girls are a daily inspiration. Not just for our personal finances, you also inspire me to be intentional about the mark I leave on this world—so you know that you can do the same. Being your mom is one of the greatest privileges of my entire life!

Right before I started this project, I heard the phrase, "there is no such thing as good writing, only good editing." I now wholeheartedly agree. I want to thank my research and editorial team members CF, JF, TS, and JPL. Thank you for transforming my writing into something impactful and coherent. I am so grateful for your talents. You each have added a unique and meaningful imprint to this book.

A special shout out to my beta reader squad! Every single word of your feedback was valuable. I am so grateful for your honesty, suggestions, advice, and encouragement. This work is so much better as a result of your generosity.

I also want to express appreciation to The Theo Group for your unwavering support of this project and co-creating the personal balance sheets. Your consistent coaching has helped us to be in the financial place that we are today. Thank you to Black Mental Wellness for providing a valuable layer of professional insight and advice regarding transforming mindsets.

Thank you to my amazing launch team! Y'all are the bomb. Your energy and excitement outweighed my nervousness and insecurities so many days. Special thanks to AB, LR, WH, TJ, DM, and MS. Thank you for being my "frens," cheerleaders, and lending your talents to help see this vision become a success. Finally, I am incredibly grateful for everyone who prayed with me or for this project. Your intercession is so precious. Please keep the prayers flowing!

To everyone who has positively touched this project in any way at any point, I thank you with immense gratitude!

Introduction

Why #7-Figure Net Worth?

> *"We should always have three friends in our lives—one who walks ahead who we look up to and follow; one who walks beside us, who is with us every step of our journey; and then, one who we reach back for and bring along after we've cleared the way."*
>
> *– Michelle Obama*

As I was getting ready to launch this book, the question of "why" I am doing this work continued arising in multiple conversations. It is an intriguing question that caused me to take a few introspective moments. I ultimately concluded that there is no single reason why I am doing this work but rather a culmination of a lifetime of experiences that led me to this moment of authorship.

My background is pretty colorful. I started my life in Los Angeles – attending top private schools. My education was funded by my mom's successful career working as a legal secretary at the top LA law firms. Then life drastically changed. My parents broke up, and my mom went through a major depression that eventually caused us to get evicted from our beautiful Mid-Wilshire apartment. After that, we bounced around for a couple of months, living with friends and in hotels. Eventually, my mom took my uncle up on his offer for us to relocate to Mississippi so we could live with family while my mom regrouped. All of this happened the summer after first grade, and I still remember that change vividly.

That shift created a new chapter in our lives. To this day, my mom calls our almost decade of living there the "Mississippi experience" because those years were economically very tough for us. Through struggles with inconsistent employment, temporary jobs, persistent mental health challenges, those were very lean years for us. My encounters with poverty were the most intense during that time. From multiple evictions to living in homes that were condemned as uninhabitable as soon as we moved out, those years were defined by what we didn't have far more than what we did. I remember days of us counting change to get a kid's meal that we would share, or days when my mom wouldn't eat at all so that I could.

The great thing about childhood naivety is that while I knew we didn't have as much as others, ours was the only world I knew, and I was happy. I praise God for His protection and His joy! I am so fortunate that the richest gift my mom gave me was the upbringing and teaching to remain deeply rooted in faith and the instruction on how to walk closely with God. That faith has indeed strengthened and sustained me. She spoke words of life to me daily and instilled confidence that I would successfully fulfill my God–given purpose. She still sends me daily texts of encouragement. My mom and I always say that while I didn't grow up with many physical possessions like clothes, toys, or gadgets. I was instead *undeniably spoiled* with an abundance of love and affirmation. These have helped shape me into the confident woman I am today.

In retrospect and examining those years, it seems starker now than it felt when we were going through it. At that time, it was simply our world. As a single parent, my mom remained committed to ensuring that my education was never affected despite our economic hardships. After two years of not being academically challenged in my local public school, my mom got fed–up. She enrolled me on a partial scholarship at one of the top private schools in our city. That year—fourth grade—was probably the genesis of my "boujetto"—a mix of boughie and ghetto or frugal and fly—self–labeled personality. A label I still use amongst my family and friends.

At home, we were juggling which utility bills to pay and what we needed to put back at the grocery store checkout. At school, I was learning and socializing with the kids of the city's elite, and I was picking up some of their tastes. Because of the things I would say at home or during phone conversations with my dad, my parents sarcastically dubbed me the "poor little rich girl." It was the dichotomy I have continued to live with to this day. It's always funny how people who meet me now or even during my college years assume that "I come from money." They are often surprised if we became close and I end up sharing my upbringing's financial reality.

It is perhaps this one foot in each world along with God's loving nudges that have equipped me to write this book. I've had first-hand exposure to a life of scarcity, lack, and poverty mindsets. I have also seen a completely different world—composed of fully-funded retirement accounts, mortgages paid off early, million-dollar businesses, and generational wealth passed down through wills and trusts.

Unfortunately, that early exposure did not translate into personal financial management knowledge or confidence. Not one of those families at my private schools ever sat me down at their dining room table. There was no conversation where they shared *how* they built the life I witnessed when I visited for playdates or sleepovers. That early exposure created a deeply rooted awareness as I walked into adulthood that there was so much I didn't know about finances. As a young adult and college graduate, I felt completely and utterly unprepared for the reality of monthly financial management. So I studied and read countless books like *Rich Dad Poor Dad, Girl Get Your Money Straight, Think and Grow Rich*, etc. Devouring those books gave me a solid foundation for my first couple of working years. I started creating monthly budgets, stacking funds into my savings account and received the benefit of my cousins allowing me to crash with them rent-free for almost a year. This period of rent-free living enabled me to purchase a condo when I was just 23 years old. I was on my way . . . or so I thought. But that good decision was followed shortly by a lot of not-so-great financial decisions.

With my newly minted condo, my mortgage payment now took up *a lot* of my monthly budget. This line item on my budget was a challenge many of my friends did not have. Most of them were renting a place with roommates or boomeranging back to their parents or other family members' homes. As for me, instead of saying no when invited, I ended up purchasing international trips and having meals out while using my credit card to pay. I ended up with credit card debt, putting my student loans on forbearance, making minimum monthly payments, and taking out an enormous amount of debt for graduate school. My credit score took hit after hit as I reverted to the bill juggling habits of my childhood.

By the time I met my husband several years later, my credit scores and financial confidence were in the tank. The housing recession hit hard and the value of my once esteemed open-air and light-filled condo plummeted. Once I added in becoming the full-time legal guardian of my high school-aged sister, my early career salary was beyond stretched thin. I was definitely in need of a reset button.

My hubby-to-be and I were always candid with each other about our finances from day one. We now laugh about how I asked him his credit score before agreeing to lunch with him. Through our transparent conversations, we both realized that neither of us had inherited financial education from our parents. We decided during our pre-marital counseling stage to change our financial tree for the better. We reviewed each other's credit reports and talked about financial approaches to checking and savings accounts. We even created a joint budget for our married life all before we said: "I do."

Committing to working toward a bright financial future was a great decision to make, but working it out in reality was a whole different animal! It took us *years* of reading books together, countless conversations (and arguments) about money, taking financial classes together, and finally hiring a financial coach before we were able to start checking off our financial goals in a meaningful way.

Though worthwhile, the process at times was surprisingly and deeply emotional. For my part, I had to challenge and tear down so many harmful mindsets that I developed while growing up and carried into adulthood. I share some of those moments of struggle throughout this book. From crying over spreadsheets as I felt inept at reconciling our budget to God lovingly but firmly coaching me to stop saying and thinking, "I'm not good with money." It required some real and, at times, gut-wrenching self-examination and super uncomfortable work of discipline to develop the slow and deliberate process of establishing new habits. There were also multiple seasons of deferred fulfillment in order to get to a place where our financial picture started to change for the better—not only in the numbers but perhaps more importantly in my soul.

My journey has taken me from the poverty and scarcity mindsets that I grew up with into the abundant mindset and solid financial foundation our family delights in today. With prayer, diligence, and persistence, today, we have been blessed to reach our first round of financial goals. Over the last few years, we were able to establish our short-term emergency savings and then our long-term emergency savings fund; pay off all of our consumer debt, including student loans that totaled over $120K; max out our annual retirement contributions, establish IRAs; save for a house down payment, and self-fund and invest in multiple businesses. Whew! Let me tell y'all! Rattling off those milestones sounds really good, but each of those semicolons represents a lot of worthwhile work from one stage to the next.

Our earnings landing us into the highest tax bracket and figuring out how to reach our initial set of financial goals has taught us so much. Far more than I communicate in these pages. However, I am going to try to share as much as I can. My goal is for *you* to know that breaking free of stagnant financial mindsets *is possible* for you too—regardless of your upbringing—low, middle class, upper-middle-class, or wealthy.

My story just happens to be one rooted in poverty. Still, some mindsets that can be detrimental to a successful financial journey are embedded at every income level of upbringing. The point is to identify these mindsets, replace them, set your own financial goals, and then chart your own path forward.

So why this book? Why this work? Why the #7-Figure Net Worth project? There are a couple reasons. First, the countless tragic events and subsequent protests in our community during 2020 caused me to become introspective about what *my* part should be in all this. I truly believe that making an impact on the black personal finance landscape in America by starting the #7-Figure Net Worth project is my current contribution. Through Yahuah's guidance and encouragement, when I sat down and thought about it, I realized there was so much I have learned about personal finance along the way that I could share.

Second, I also realized there are not many books or curriculums targeting black Americans that provide a mix of foundational *and* intermediate financial strategies. There is a need for more education aimed at those of us who may have achieved or are en route to attaining mid to high incomes. I realized that we black middle and upper-middle-class folks also need a financial roadmap. Our challenges, obstacles, and opportunities look and feel substantially different than many of our white counterparts with similar earning potential.

This work was born from *that* place. It is for my children and yours to start their financial journeys at a more empowering place than we did. There is value in re-tracing the steps we have taken in order to carve a more defined path for those who may be interested in a similar blueprint for their own lives. This book is my labor of love, my transparency, and me being willing to share—even though our #7-Figure Net Worth journey is still a work in progress. It's me creating the de-tailed #BlackMillenialAdulting step-by-step roadmap that I wish someone could have handed me when I first started.

To be raw-level transparent, this is definitely *not* a work I even *wanted* to do. I even ran from it for a while. I ran because I didn't feel qualified *at all* to teach *anyone* about finances.

However, Yahuah has lovingly affirmed throughout this process that He doesn't call the qualified. He qualifies the called. So I hope that this blueprint is a blessing to you and your future generations. As I share my journey, I hope to create a road-map for many of my melanin brothers and sisters to follow and for future gener-ations to benefit from. I want to illuminate a path you can follow where the goal is not attaining a 6-figure income. The path is to the elevated goal of leveraging your income to gain a #7-Figure Net Worth and create generational wealth. Shift your mindset accordingly.

I hope you opt to undertake or continue along this journey. May enduring wealth become your and your family's portion, in agreement with Proverbs 8:18 KJV, "Riches and honour *are* with me; *yea*, durable riches, and righteousness."

May you be challenged, empowered, and encouraged on your financial journey.

Brielle Mabrey

The #7-Figure Net Worth Blueprint

Y ou may have picked up this book or downloaded an electronic copy because there was something about your finances that you want to tweak, transform, or change. This may be your first financial read or perhaps you are an avid reader of financial education books. Maybe you weren't the one who purchased it and someone decided to give it to you. Regardless of how or why you arrived at this page, I'm so grateful you did.

While this work is written with black American millennials readers in mind, there are aspects of this work that can apply across various age groups, ethnicities, and stages of life. This book may also serve different roles, depending on your financial background and knowledge. For some, it may provide a new and comprehensive oversight to help you jumpstart your journey to wealth. For others, you may glean a couple of new ideas to fine-tune your current path. There may be very high-income readers who have been in their careers for 10+ years but haven't yet acquired core foundational financial knowledge. Others may be in their first job but have been reading finance books since their teens and are just looking for additional practical suggestions.

Given the wide variance, I do my best in this work to cover foundational financial principles while also providing guidance on intermediate-level financial strategies. My goal in this work is to provide you with tools, thoughts, and concepts that can help you design *or* affirm your journey to a #7-Figure Net Worth.

Here's the deal, though. This book is not a handful of steps that you can take to become a millionaire overnight. Before you invest any more of your time to read another word, let me ensure that I make that clear.

This book provides mindsets, practical actions, and disciplined habits that you can implement to attain a #7-Figure Net Worth over time! Have you maybe just considered closing the book? I don't blame you. Action and discipline may not sound the most appealing *at first*. I vastly underestimated the internal and external work that would be necessary to achieve financial success. With this book, the great news is that in these pages you will receive a blueprint with clear steps that you can take to create your own journey. This blueprint will provide you with a hybrid of sociological context, financial insight and education, and action-enabling worksheets. The combination of financial insight and actionable worksheets will propel you towards your financial goals step-by-step. Knowledge plus action! We're in this together.

While focused primarily on personal action and habits, this book also examines the unique wealth challenges black Americans face. Let's be real. As black Americans, we often have a complex and, at times, pretty funky relationship with money. Countless things are standing in the way of us building and retaining wealth, including our cultural norms, systemic racism, interdependent personal relationships, workplace battles, disparate health outcomes, banking and housing discrimination . . . and the list goes on. If Black America and Wealth were in a relationship on Facebook, suffice it to say that the status would definitely be, "It's complicated."

Our history *and* social structures have woven together to impact the financial experience of today's modern black American. In this work, we'll look at some of the macro-level factors that affect us while also breaking down micro-level actions that we can take despite and perhaps even in protest of those macro influences.

While it is important to be *aware* of the factors that influence your pocketbooks, you don't have to be *defined* by it. You have the ability through your mindsets and daily habits to build a vibrant financial future and attain a #7-Figure Net Worth despite these challenges. Let me show you how.

How to Leverage this Blueprint

There are multiple approaches that you can take to leveraging this resource in your life.

HOW

Read Through Completely and Circle Back

One approach to using this resource may be to read through the entire book and then circle back and work through the worksheets one-by-one.

Step-by-Step

Another option may be to read a section, digest it, and immediately complete the corresponding worksheets. If you follow this approach, it may help to establish a schedule. For example, you may say that you will read this book every day at 7 pm and do the worksheets until you finish. Another option may be to commit that every Saturday for the next ___ weeks. You could dedicate one hour to read through two sections and complete the corresponding worksheets. Do what will work best for you.

WHO

With Accountability Partner(s)

Personal finance has a lot in common with other personal disciplines, like eating healthy and exercise. Countless studies have shown that we are more likely to reach our goals when we create accountability. You may find it helpful to identify someone or a small group of people to digest and work through this book with you. Who comes to mind for you? You may want to reach out to see if they want to partner up with you to enhance their personal financial profile. If you need help finding a partner, feel free to post in our #7-Figure Net Worth Facebook group to see if there is someone interested in being a virtual partner to you.

With a Small Group

Whether through your church, a book club, or another group you are a part of, this may be a great resource to bring to a group and set a cadence for reading, discussing, and working through the worksheets.

With a Financial Coach

This could be a resource that you also use while working with a personal financial coach. It can be a great supplement to the resources they may provide and help you identify topics you want to discuss during your coaching sessions. They can also offer professional insight on key aspects of the blueprint that you design.

With a Financial Advisor

This could be a resource you use while also working with a financial advisor. A financial advisor can fine-tune your blueprint and be a knowledgeable resource to help you with the granular details of your plan, especially related to investing.

If you are not yet working with a financial coach or financial advisor, no worries. We will talk more about the role that each can play in your financial journey.

WHAT

Supplies

I also suggest you keep a highlighter and pencil handy when reading through this blueprint. I recommend that you grab a physical folder to place your relevant financial documents in. If you are using a computer, create a folder in the cloud or locally. Place any financial documents you may need to keep track of in a digital format in that folder.

Regardless of your approach, I hope this resource is a blessing to your life and allows you to refine and improve your personal finance landscape.

Parts of the #7-Figure Net Worth Blueprint

Now let's talk about the framework for this conversation we are about to have. This blueprint is rooted in the biblical concepts of wisdom and financial stewardship. It will help you get your numbers, habits, mindsets, and legacy in harmony so you can build or reinforce a strong financial house. If you can be honest, intentional, and disciplined in these four areas, I believe you can improve your financial landscape. While a strategic focus on these four areas may not be the only path to financial success, it is the blueprint that I'm excited to share with you in the following pages.

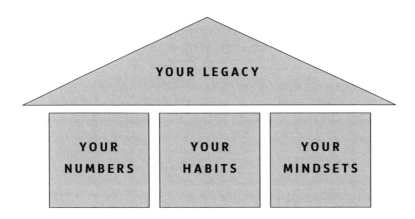

1. Your Numbers – In the first steps of this blueprint, we will calculate your current net worth to get a clear numerical picture of where you are today. We will take a close look at all of your income sources, assets, investments, and debts and liabilities.

Once you know where you are, we will take some time to dream about where you want to be. We will walk through the steps to set baseline goals and stretch goals about what you want your financial future and that of your future generations to look like.

Next, we will go deep into your financial details—digging into the numbers related to your insurance portfolio and your paycheck deductions and employee benefits—where applicable. We want to be sure to account for every dollar that can be put to work on your wealth goals.

2. Your Habits – Second, I'll help you get honest about the impact of your daily, weekly, and monthly decisions on your ability to reach your financial goals. We will talk about the foundational habits of financial success, including budgeting and reconciling, creating multiple income streams, saving intentionally, giving impactfully, investing, and more. You will be empowered to infuse your life with habits that are in alignment with your financial goals.

3. Your Mindsets – Third, we will examine your money mindsets. I'll provide you with strategies to replace stagnant money mindsets with healthy thoughts of abundance and attainable goals.

This section will also examine your relationship with money and your relation-ships with people that involve money. *Spoiler alert*: reaching your financial goals may mean you may have to cut some people off. Yep, I said it . . . just like that! Sometimes when you are the constant source of $100 here and there—you may be siphoning off funds that can create an intergenerational financial legacy.

Together, we will take a hard look at your relationships that include financial support and identify the ones you want to be intentional about and keep. For the ones you opt to keep, we'll create some boundaries and rules of engagement about the financial support you provide.

4. Your Legacy – Finally, we will take a moment to reflect on the legacy that you desire to build. We will also work on organizing key documents that are es-sential to passing down generational wealth.

Now that we have this four-part framework let's get ready for some details. Architecture makes us aware that just having the blueprint for a home is not the same as building the house. In the chapters that follow, we will talk about the wisdom, strategy, and action needed to utilize this blueprint to build, maintain, or renovate your financial house. "Through skillful and godly Wisdom is a house (a life, a home, a family) built and by understanding is it established (on a sound and good foundation). And by knowledge shall its chambers (of every area) be filled with all precious and pleasant riches" (Proverbs 24:3–4 AMP).

Now, let me tell you right away. I will *not* cover every aspect of the financial strategies that could be a component of your financial journey in granular detail in this book. For some topics, I may cover a particular aspect and then provide you with supplementary resource suggestions that may offer a more detailed and comprehensive coverage on that topic. My goal in crafting this book is to provide an aggregate resource that presents an attainable path and culturally augment some of the existing work in the market on these topics. Remember, this book is a roadmap—not the full encyclopedia of all things black folks and financial.

With that in mind, if you are ready to swing that hammer and put in the real work, let's get started!

Your Numbers
Financial Assets

> *Some people pretend to be rich,*
> *but have nothing.*
> *Others pretend to be poor,*
> *but own a fortune.*
>
> *– Proverbs 13:7 (Good News Translation)*

N ot too long ago, the picture of millionaire soccer star Sadio Mane's cracked phone went viral. How is it that a man with an annual salary eclipsing $10 million can walk around with a cracked iPhone screen— and not even the latest version, at that?

Priorities, man(e)!

"I do not need (to have) luxury cars, luxury homes, trips (or) even planes," Mane said in an interview with the Daily Star. Mane is just one example of countless millionaires walking around in t-shirts, jeans, and non-designer shoes. But . . . what about us? Can we each make material sacrifices in pursuit of lasting inter-generational wealth?

Let me be clear—there is nothing wrong with buying nice items and looking good. I know that many of us want the latest and greatest of everything and, for most of us, it is well deserved. However, it is all about prioritization and the order of asset accumulation.

I'm sure many of us have personal or friends and family with "struggle stories" about how we came up. Well, let me speak for myself. As a latch key kid—I have definitely heated up more ramen noodle meals than I can count on a two-burner electric stove. The electric stove was often powered by an extension cord that ran from my neighbor's house because our power had been disconnected. Miraculously, no one was hurt throughout that process, but the struggle was indeed real.

So how does that relate to assets? For many of us, now that we've gained that high five-, six-, or even seven-figure salary, we want to splurge. I get it! For those who may have grown up in a solid middle or upper-middle-class family, you may still have a desire to maintain the finer things in life by driving the newest luxury cars, wearing the latest fashions, or owning the latest gadgets. In some of us, the spending splurge or "de-serve" is exceptionally strong. We want everything now because our upbringing was financially difficult. In other cases, it may just be the lifestyle you grew up with.

Regardless of our economic backgrounds or financial history, you can transform your economic standing. To do so, it is important to intentionally note the financial resources that you spend towards appreciating and depreciating assets, respectively. Well, what's the difference? A depreciating asset is something that you own or purchase that decreases in value over time. Examples include vehicles, clothing, toys, gadgets, electronics, furniture, decor, and other similar items (unless an antique or collector's item which can hold or appreciate in value). Depreciation comes from accounting terms, which mean physical and tangible assets whose cost is calculated given limited usefulness over a specific period.

For example, if you buy an outfit online for $120, wear it 6–7 times, then a year later, when you sell it on eBay or at a consignment store, you may only get a small fraction of what you paid for it. Let's say $40. That value has depreciated by $80 in that period. If you wait two years, that outfit may be out of style and you may not be able to sell it at all—depreciating to a value of $0. This change in value from the amount initially paid to a much lower value applies to many items in the depreciating asset category.

On the other hand, appreciating assets are items that you buy, invest in or own that increase in value over time like your 401(k), IRA, real estate, mutual funds, stocks, bonds, or a business. You could even have collector's items such as jewelry, art, vintage items, or other valuables that are worth a substantial and increasing amount of money. For example, a person can purchase a renaissance painting for $2.3 million. Five years later, it is assessed for an increased value of $7.4 million.

I understand that the temptation is strong for many of us to use our financial resources to purchase depreciating assets or things that decrease in value over time. It may even be rooted in a desire to show our success to others. Societal norms, advertising, and social media do not make it easy to resist. However, there may be a point where you stop showing success from the outside in and instead put a higher priority on building generational wealth from the inside out.

Focusing solely on decorating our life with depreciating assets is a lot like living at the fiscal edge. It works for a while—may even feel great until an opportunity or incident demands our attention—and we need to contribute significantly to something. We may then find ourselves scraping the bottom of our wallets or banking accounts to address a situation because we have not set aside an emergency or "rainy day" savings fund or invested in appreciating assets—things that increase in value over time that we could have been able to liquidate.

In those moments, we may find ourselves hoping and wishing we had allocated your resources differently. Perhaps, allocating our money toward income-generating assets like stocks or real estate instead of making a down payment on a brand-new car that depreciated significantly the moment we drove it off the lot. The moment we come to that realization may look different for all of us. It could be a health crisis, a job layoff, a loved one facing eviction, or something else that causes you to tap into an emergency fund of cash or liquid assets. It could even be a positive moment like an opportunity to invest in an up and coming business or a child getting admitted to an elite school that requires tuition payments when you wish that you had more appreciating assets available. The great news is that you don't have to wait for *that* next moment. You can make key changes now!

Referring to the picture of Sadio Mane's cracked phone, a person tweeted, "The goal is not to look rich, but to *be* rich silently." Now, how do you get to a point where you can silently make your moves to better sustain your future as opposed to spending your hard-earned money on depreciating assets?

Shift away from using your income to acquire things you or others can immediately touch or feel as your measurement for financial success. **Change to using**

your personal net worth and balance sheet as the way you identify strong financial health and status. A personal balance sheet will give you an overall view of your assets at a point in time and summarizes your net worth by adding your assets (what you own) and subtracting your liabilities (what you owe). When you view your status and financial success from that perspective, it can change the way you use your money.

Wise decisions today can transform your current and future financial circumstances. Integrate a greater awareness of the type of assets you use your hard-earned dollars toward. Shift your focus from what you can *make* to what you can *grow and keep*. Think carefully before pulling out your card to swipe or before typing it in—knowing that each purchase either <u>contributes</u> *or* <u>detracts</u> from your personal net worth. Alternatively, when you live as though "tomorrow" does not exist, your bank account and, more importantly, your personal balance sheet will eventually show it.

As I said before, I am not saying that expensive cars, recreational vehicles, clothes, electronics, or all of these things won't fit into your lifestyle at some point. However, I am saying there should be a thoughtful sequence to the stage of your journey when these items are purchased. **Priorities, man.** You can choose to indulge in *some* of those items that may not hold long-term value ***after*** accomplishing specific financial goals that you define. For example, you may defer a luxury car purchase until after you achieve a certain net worth, pay off a certain amount of debt, or achieve a certain balance in your retirement account. The key is planning, balance and foresight. Keep in mind that "foresight will protect you. Understanding will guard you" (Proverbs 2:11 GWT).

Now, let's take a look at the first half of your net worth calculation—your assets. For this first worksheet, we will take a close look at all of your current assets. We will examine what you have currently accumulated and what is allocated between appreciating and depreciating assets. We want to get a snapshot of where you are and identify where you would like to go. Let's get to it!

Your Numbers
Financial Assets

. . . .

PLEASE LIST THE NUMERICAL VALUE OF YOUR TOTAL ASSETS IN THE FOLLOWING CATEGORIES

				TOTAL
CASH	_____	_____	_____	_____
CHECKING	_____	_____	_____	_____
SAVINGS	_____	_____	_____	_____
CERTIFICATE OF DEPOSITS	_____	_____	_____	_____

INVESTMENT ACCOUNTS

					TOTAL
IRA	_____	_____	_____	_____	_____
MUTUAL FUND	_____	_____	_____	_____	_____
401K	_____	_____	_____	_____	_____
503B	_____	_____	_____	_____	_____
STOCKS	_____	_____	_____	_____	_____
OTHER	_____	_____	_____	_____	_____

OTHER ASSET TYPES

			TOTAL
CASH VALUE INSURANCE POLICIES	_____	_____	_____
ANGEL INVESTMENTS	_____	_____	_____
BUSINESS EQUITY	_____	_____	_____
ART	_____	_____	_____
CRYPTOCURRENCY	_____	_____	_____
REAL ESTATE (ONLY INCLUDE CURRENT VALUE MINUS ANY OUTSTANDING LOAN AMOUNT)	_____	_____	_____
VEHICLES (ONLY INCLUDE CURRENT VALUE MINUS ANY OUTSTANDING LOAN AMOUNT)	_____	_____	_____
OTHER	_____	_____	_____

TOTAL VALUE OF ASSETS _____

CHAPTER TWO

Your Numbers
Financial Liabilities & Debt

> *"What I am about to share, you would do well to write on your heart and place in your purse. Many a ruined man dates his downfall from the day he began buying what he did not need. If you are in debt, part of you belongs to your creditors. To whom you give your money, you give your power."*
>
> *– W.E.B. Dubois as quoted by Dennis Kimbro, The Wealth Choice, Success Secrets of Black Millionaires*

"See the way that my checking and savings is set up!" I know many of y'all have either heard or said that statement. We may say it when we have too many debits hitting, when we want to find our way out of paying for something or insert your own personal scenario. For too many black Americans, the truth of that statement is that a checking and savings account may be the only or primary financial tool we use.

As we focus on increasing your personal net worth, the financial tools that will be a part of your arsenal will expand. When focused on net worth, the tools that many businesses use will begin to have an application to your personal financial portfolio. We move from checking and savings accounts to personal balance sheets and personal cash flow statements.

Let's talk about personal cash flow statements. A personal cash flow statement calculates the cash that flows into your hands (money you earn) as well as the cash that leaves your hands (money you spend) to see if you keep a positive or negative impact and balance with each transaction. The key for personal cash flow is to ensure you always have funds remaining after every transaction—which is an example of positive cash flow.

It is similar to a personal balance sheet. The goal will be to continually decrease your debt and liabilities and increase the value of your assets to achieve a positive net worth and grow it to a million dollars and beyond. When it comes to personal finance, we often hear the term "debt" far more often than "liability." However, liability is the broader category that debt falls within.

Liabilities can include any type of financial obligation we incur. Examples include income taxes, bills we need to pay, or services we agree to perform that have an associated value. Debt is created when something specific is borrowed—typically money. If you ask someone to let you hold $100 until you get paid next week, and they give it to you, you are now in debt to that person for $100. The same is true if you gain a car loan or mortgage from a bank, a student loan request to the Department of Education, or a credit card from a financial services company. These are all common examples of debt.

Let's talk more about the big "d" word—DEBT. It is often the cause of *negative* net worth. It can also be a heavy topic for many of us. For some, this topic may trigger emotions of weight, burden, exhaustion, and hopelessness. For others, it may trigger guilt, shame, and embarrassment. Some may have been taught early on about the dangers of debt and successfully avoided incurring debt in our adult lives. For others, it may just be "it is what it is" and has just become an accepted part of life.

Regardless, if the presence of debt in your life ignites you to "go get it gone" and repay it quickly or causes you to roll your eyes in exasperation, it is something the majority of black Americans will have to deal with at some point in our personal financial journeys. For example, acquiring real estate, starting a new business or buying an existing one, or even obtaining higher education that can lead to a higher salary—for us, often begins with a loan.

When it comes to most financial debt, there are typically two components—the principal and interest. The principal is the initial amount borrowed. The interest is the additional amount being charged to you to borrow that money. It is typically expressed as a percentage and is also described as an annual percentage rate (APR).

Now, some may consider all forms of debt to be negative. Those of this mind may firmly believe that purchasing everything with the cash you have is the way to go. Others believe that certain types of debt can be positive. What's the difference? Let me share.

In most financial circles, negative debt would be considered obligations incurred to purchase items that will not retain their value over time—depreciating assets. Positive debt would be obligations incurred to purchase assets that will hold or increase their value over time—appreciating assets. Positive debt would also include debt that is incurred to create leverage for creating earning potential such as business loans, and in some cases, student loans. I will focus in more detail on student loans in a subsequent section.

However, not all debt is negative. For example, buying a home or pursuing a college education can provide economic mobility in many (but not all) cases. These are debts that have the potential of increasing your net worth over time. The key here is to ensure you receive at least a decent interest rate and favorable repayment terms when you take out a loan for things like that. Negative debt often involves borrowing or spending money to purchase depreciating assets like a vehicle or clothing.

Loan Discrimination

While "good debt" is something to work for, discriminatory lending practices have even impeded many black Americans' progress with converting "good debt" into positive gains in our net worth.

After evaluating nearly 7 million 30-year mortgages, a recent University of California at Berkeley study reported that black and Latino applicants were charged both higher interest rates and refinance fees than white borrowers.

That data evaluated face-to-face transactions and showed that fees still were more when minorities applied online or through an app. One researcher cited an example of a black homeowner with a $429,000 mortgage–paying an average of $640 more over the life of that loan.

Additionally, a 2018 Lending Tree study reported that black Americans had the highest denial rates at 17.4 percent. Whereas white applicants had the lowest denial rates at 7.9%. The study noted a persistent trend as black and Latino applicants consistently endured the highest denial rates for the previous 14 years.

Mortgage loans are not the only places that black Americans see discriminatory practices. An investigation by the National Fair Housing Alliance found that applicants who were people of color, and more financially qualified, were offered higher–priced car loans 60 percent of the time. This translated to cost an extra $2,662 throughout the loan!

These discriminatory practices prompted the proposal of the Loan Shark Prevention Act, enabled to combat the predatory lending practices of America's largest banks. The goal is to protect the consumers who are already burdened with exorbitant credit–card interest rates—capping interest rates at 15 percent.

Some laws that prevent credit discrimination are already in place. But just as we've seen and read before, there are banks and loan companies that will figure out a way around it—for whatever reason. While unfair practices can try to stifle our ability to obtain "good debt," there is an abundance of opportunities for us to collect "bad debt."

Predatory Loans

Payday loans. Subprime mortgages and auto loans. Rent-to-Own Furniture. Title Loans. They are called predatory loans for a good reason. They prey on those who desperately need help or can't look anywhere else to find a loan. You will generally find these subprime lenders attached to vehicles or scattered throughout the hood in the form of payday and title loans. Why are they in the hood? Because they expect us to fall in hard times, run out of options, and then fall into the trap of inexplicably high–interest rate loans and fees once we walk out of the building.

On average, the interest rate for one payday loan is **391 percent**—and that is if you pay it back in two weeks. Suppose you can't repay the loans (the Consumer

Financial Protection Bureau notes that 80 percent of payday loans are not repaid within two weeks). In that case, your interest rate jumps to 521 percent! It continually increases if you can't repay the debt within the period. If you add a coupl payday loans with a subprime auto loan, you could be looking at a dark financial hole that you'd be hard-pressed to burrow out of.

In the financial circle of life, many things begin with creditworthiness and end with loans. Far too many black Americans may end up "stuck" with these types of extremely high-interest loan options because that is all their credit can warrant. Your credit score can be a critical factor in determining your ability to take out a loan. This can in turn, have positive (if you leverage it to increase the value of your assets) or negative impacts on your net worth (if you expend that debt for depreciating assets).

Now, that is not to say that you don't have a level of personal responsibility when it comes to your creditworthiness. You definitely do! If your credit is in bad shape, there are many things you can do to reverse its direction. We will talk about some of those basic strategies later on in this book.

If this cycle of predatory lending is one that you currently find yourself in, don't get discouraged. You can break free of this cycle! The habits and strategies discussed in subsequent sections can help you achieve positive cash flow, and hopefully, over time eliminate any need to use this type of predatory financial product.

American Debt Landscape

Now don't get me wrong— even though I am contrasting the difference, I'm not saying that "bad debt" or even consumer debt is only a black American problem. Debt is definitely a widespread American problem, point blank "periodt." A 13.5 trillion-dollar problem, to be exact. In 2018, NerdWallet reported that when you combined mortgages, credit cards, student and auto loans, Americans' aggregate debt amounted to this number. That is more than a 10 percent increase from five years ago.

However, debt *is* a problem that impacts our communities and our culture with greater frequency and often more dire outcomes. The American societal context that we live in means that, by default, most black Americans don't have the same financial cushion as white Americans. This means we are more likely to use debt to make ends meet.

Limited financial resources also mean that we struggle more than our white counterparts to repay that debt. Many of us know the drill. You, a parent, a friend, or a loved one sit at the kitchen table, placing bills in order of importance. "Well, I've got a few more weeks before this gets cut off, so I can wait—I can use that money to go ahead and pay this other bill." In the end, we rob Peter to pay Paul—which often just digs us further into a hole. We get used to that juggle with rent and utility bills, so we "think" we can do it with debt as well, but the consequences are far more severe.

Another study reported that nationally only 15 percent of white households were late paying their debts compared to more than 27 percent of black house-holds. This was the case even though the median debt for black Americans was only $30,800 compared to the white median debt of $73,800 – which is less than half! This gap was also true when it came to good credit – with 40 percent of black households compared to 65 percent of white households reporting good or excellent credit.

For black Americans, our debt situations are not always solely because of an individual lack of responsibility. Many of us do take the proper action to correct and eradicate our debt. However, in many situations, individual debt is being compounded by generations of discriminatory practices. Then when this debt also produces bad credit, the struggle for financial freedom intensifies. So, we tend to do whatever we can to get what we need. Often, it lands us into a worse situation and can often become a generational struggle. Let me give you a scenario that may sound familiar.

Debt as an inheritance

Let's take a look at Lisa's situation.

Lisa is a single mom of two teenage boys—ages 16 and 18. Her divorce six months ago has left her with a lot of credit card debt and a very low credit score. Even though she has a pretty good salary, keeping up in a high-cost-of-living area with bills while feeding two growing teenage boys had been a struggle. With her ex-husband unemployed and no child support coming in the past four months, things have gotten even tighter. She's had to juggle bills, miss payments, even go into default on one account—tanking her credit scores even more.

To try and loosen the financial strain, Lisa decided to move into a more affordable two-bedroom apartment and have the boys share a room. When the time comes to get her utilities turned on, she gets denied. Frustrated, she uses her oldest son's social security number to get cable and electricity service in his name. She rationalizes that it's okay because she is just doing what she has to do. Thinking to herself, "I" ll never get behind on my utility payments, so no harm will be done." At this moment, Lisa doesn't really look ahead to what will happen a few months or years later if money gets really tight again. Especially without an emergency fund in place to be able to pay the bill. She did recall hearing her younger cousin complain that when he was 22, he tried to buy a car and couldn't get approval for the loan. His credit was bad from his mom having unpaid utility bills in his name. She brushes this thought aside as she fills out the paperwork.

Listen—I'm not sharing this story to pass judgment on Lisa or anyone else who has done what they had to do to make it work. Her story hits way too close to home for me to do that. Times get hard—trust me, I know it. You end up taking debt on top of debt when situations crop up that you do not have the cash to cover. **I do share it to illustrate that our decisions as they relate to debt can have an inter-generational impact.** We should be aware of it and mindful to use proactive strategies, like setting up emergency savings funds, whenever possible. Now, let's talk about another reason why *avoiding* debt is critical for modern black Americans.

Get Yo' Hands Out My Pocket

If the trend of depreciating assets comprising the majority of our debt, higher default rates, and higher interest rates for the same financial products were not enough, black Americans *also* face a completely different experience when it comes to debt collection. We are more likely to be sued to collect the debt owed.

Experts cite many reasons why black Americans might face more lawsuits than white Americans. Still, the main reason lies in the immense financial resources gap between the two demographics. "I'm in a generational hole," said Miranda Jones, a city council member, and executive with Better Family Lives. She and her husband have been sued three times in recent years over debts—once resulting in the seizure of $800 from her bank account.

There is very little protection from a policy and legal perspective from situations like the one that Miranda and her family encountered. Federal law and most state laws protect only the poorest of the poor from having their wages seized. Otherwise, the law allows plaintiffs to seize up to a quarter of a worker's after-tax pay. ProPublica's analysis of five years of court judgments from three metropolitan areas—St. Louis, Chicago, and Newark—showed that even accounting for income, the rate of judgments was twice as high in mostly black neighborhoods as primarily white ones.

So What's the Lesson?

What do we learn from all of this? There are three clear lessons I see for black Americans here. You may see additional ones, but these are my initial three.

"Ain't nobody got time for that." While I will cover intentional savings and building emergency funds in more detail later in the book, I have to also mention it here. When the alternative is credit card debt or car title and payday loans with exorbitant interest rates, it becomes an urgent need for black Americans to establish at least a baseline emergency fund of $1,000. If you are sitting there saying, "That sounds great, but you don't know my life," you are right. There may need to be some changes—whether income, expense, or mindset—made before you get there. You may have to approach this in small steps. Also, you may want to google "Dave Ramsey emergency fund." There are stories and strategies from people of all starting points on how they got creative to get their first emergency fund in place.

"We have gots to be more careful!" Now, usually, when someone says that, it is in a joking manner. I am so serious here. For black Americans, the cost of debt is extremely high, so we, more than other groups, have to be extremely careful

about what we incur debt for. Using a credit card to purchase depreciating assets such as meals, clothes, jewelry, electronics, etc. is a luxury that we cannot afford. It is a practice that literally can cost us more.

"We gotta play chess, not checkers." We *have to* wise up on our strategic moves when leveraging "positive" debt to create income-producing and appreciating assets. We have to play the game differently than we have been—getting off the checkerboard and jumping up to chess. *If*—and that is a big *if* with multiple caveats—*if* black Americans choose to use debt-generating financial products, we should do all things possible to use it only when tied to an intentional and written strategy. This strategy should outline how the debt will create additional income streams or enhance our earning potential, the repayment terms, and the time frame.

Understand for us, the stakes are way higher when it comes to debt. Once the modern black American gets buried in debt, it can start a very tough cycle to get out of. Tough, but not impossible. It *is* possible to become "debt-free" with acquired wisdom, a clear plan, updated mindsets, and good habits. My husband and I climbed out of over $120k worth of debt. Whatever your number—so can you. We will talk about specific debt reduction strategies in the **Habits** section. If you are already debt-free, congrats! If you haven't yet achieved that goal, let's get into your business and look at your liabilities and debts with this next worksheet.

Your Numbers
Liabilities + Debt Dashboard

. . . .

TYPE OF DEBT	ENTITY	TOTAL OUTSTANDING	MINIMIUM MONTHLY PAYMENT	INTEREST RATE
				TOTAL DEBT LIABILITIES

Student Loan Debt

Do y'all remember when the Obamas announced that they paid off their student loans in their 40s? As someone who admires them, I gasped at the thought of the first African American president and the first lady working for decades in law and politics while still making those final loan payments. At the time, I was groaning at the ridiculous monthly payments I made each month to "Sallie Mae," trying to get my own student loan debt paid off. Their words and that mountain of debt in my own life hit home. Why is student loan debt so real for many African Americans? Even though there are various types of debts, student loans seem to disproportionately affect wealth attainment in young black Americans compared to our white counterparts. This is why I wanted to call out this type of debt in additional detail.

Now let's take a look at this statistically, based on some key metrics outlined in a 2019 Forbes article, "Millennial Student Debt Across Demographics."

While possessing less family wealth, on average 17 percent more black Americans use borrowed funds than white Americans towards bachelor's degrees.

Black millennials, on average, have $31,000 in student debt for bachelor's degrees compared to white millennials who have $26,726.

Black students disproportionately attend for-profit colleges compared to white students. It is at a rate of 13%, while only 4% of white students attend similar institutions.

Nearly 1/3 of black families have education loans (31%) compared to 1/5 (20%) of white families, even though black Americans often attend college at a lower rate than white Americans.

Sadly, black **graduates** are more likely to default on student loans than a white student that dropped out. That is hurtful because statistically speaking students, who do not finish college, often default. If black Americans are graduating yet still defaulting, what does this say about the job market? *Is it easier for a white dropout to obtain employment than a black graduate?*

These statistics' underpinnings are inextricably tied with discrimination both in wages and in the labor markets that black graduates face. I do not share these statistics to simply point out a problem. Instead, I ask all of us to face these stats boldly to better understand the macro context of the seemingly individual issues we face. We must also ask challenging questions. How can we game plan to mitigate the factors that threaten to hinder black graduates from wealth attainment after graduation? How can we address these factors in our own personal financial journey?

In such a construct, now more than ever, a significant part of the answer must be to educate ourselves about the return on investment of higher education options and related student loan products. To be transparent, it was not until I was less than a year away from completing my student loan payments that I really started to understand all of the jargon associated with student loan products. With a greater understanding from the beginning, I could have undoubtedly saved thousands of dollars using better repayment options. This would have also created the opportunity to strategically invest much earlier.

So I want to challenge you to learn *now* what I didn't know until later. To overcome our "current situation" as it relates to student loan debt, we have to equip ourselves with a keen understanding of key financial concepts related to student loans. Understand how interest and capitalization work, how payments are applied, and the important distinction between principal and interest.

Our willingness to gain wisdom and "get put on" now about the details related to student loan debt also has a real impact on intergenerational wealth. There is a literal and practical impact. I can tell you straight up that I did not contribute a dime to my kid's custodial accounts or 529 plans until we had our own student loan debts paid off first. I'm not saying that was right or wrong. Just providing a practical example of how difficult it is to build for the future when you are still paying for your past.

Can you relate to this? I vividly remember how long it took to make all my student loan payments. It baffled me that such debt was possible. This is why I feel that one of the first steps in your black adulting experience may be to understand the way loan interest impacts your repayment plan. You have to get beyond just defaulting to the lowest monthly payment possible. A larger monthly student loan payment may, in fact, be the best choice for you to reach your wealth goals. It may require making tough lifestyle choices—at least initially for a few years—so that you can maximize your payments and push those loans out of your way.

Now, keep in mind that some financial advisors will steer you away from being in a rush to repay all your student loans. I would only slow down if you have an extremely low interest rate and have a sound correlated investing plan in place.

Suppose someone can show you how to use the funds you will spend paying down student loan principal for a disciplined investment strategy instead. In that case, you may gain greater long-term financial returns with that approach. Otherwise, push ahead and remove the debt. There is no one size fits all approach. Before you decide on either strategy, I suggest that you run the numbers for each scenario and then decide what will work best for you.

My point is not to advocate for a specific approach but rather to underline that you must be intentional **and** educated when addressing student loans. Rather than sitting on autopilot, become aggressive with monthly payments, and get rid of debt quickly. If the numbers make sense for you, and you remain disciplined in routing that money as designed, go for the deferred investment route. But hear me well – if you are going to be out there—coking and joking with that money—then you are better off buckling down and getting through the self-depriving process of paying off those loans as quickly as possible.

Remember, what we model is what our babies will see! Our children must know that finances, especially university financial aid, is not free money! I recall a past decision to use student loans to stay on campus an extra semester. I wince when I think back on how I used my refund check any way I saw fit. That money came with a hefty price in the following years. If we are not careful, ineffectively managing our student loan repayment process will lower our net worth over time by increasing our debt load and reducing the capital we have available to invest.

We cannot be haphazard or lackadaisical with our future. Let's take some intentional steps with this next worksheet to understand the core aspects of your current student loan situation. We will also identify ways you can address this aspect of your life. If you don't have any student loans, congrats! Perhaps reach out to someone who is still actively paying their student loans and encourage them to pick up this book before heading to the next chapter. For those of you still trying to give Fannie Mae and 'nem the boot, let's get to this worksheet!

Your Numbers
Student Loan Debt

. . . .

Here is a list of key terms that I encourage you to gain a strong understanding of as it relates to student loan debt. Take a moment and type the following into a search engine along with the word "student loan" or "student" as appropriate.

- Loan Servicer
- Loan Cancellation
- Loan Discharge
- Grace Period
- Forgiveness
- Deferment

- Forbearance
- Federal Student Loan
- Private Student Loan
- Flexible Repayment Plans
- Capitalization of Unpaid Interest

- Direct Subsidized
- Direct Unsubsidized
- Direct PLUS
- Loan Consolidation
- Loan Refinancing

This is not a comprehensive list but should get you started on the process of gaining a more detailed understanding of how the student loan industry works. If you want to make the minimum monthly payment on your student loans and invest the difference, I encourage you to work closely with a financial coach or advisor to craft that strategy.

On the previous Debt Dashboard worksheet, you listed all of your loans and the associated interest rate. Now, let's take a closer look at your student loans.

1. What type of student loans do you have: federal, private, or both? Knowing what you know now, would you choose the same loan option? Why or why not?

2. What is the current interest rate(s) for your loan(s)?

3. What payment plan are you currently utilizing for your student loans? If you are currently not paying down your loans with a payment plan, what adjustments do you need to make in your budget to be able to set up a payment plan? Which payment plan will you choose?

4. If you continue your current plan, how much will you pay in principal and interest over the life of this loan?

5. What is the difference between that total cost and the initial amount borrowed? After seeing this difference, how does it make you feel?

6. Is there another plan that you could select that will lower the total cost of your loan? Do your research and see what your payment amount would be.

7. What, if any, budget adjustments would you need to make to be able to make that new payment amount?

8. Does your loan servicer offer a lower interest rate incentive if you enroll in automatic debits? If so, and you can budget for it, take the necessary steps to set up the automatic payments.

9. Write down the names of the high school students in your life. Who can benefit from your student loan experience and knowledge of the system? As they consider college as the next step in their lives, have a conversation with them and their parents (not all parents are experienced or knowledgeable about student loans) about the student loan process. Be an available resource for them, however, and whenever you can.

CHAPTER THREE

Your Numbers
Personal Net Worth

> "But it ain't what you cop.
> It's about what you keep."
>
> – Lauryn Hill, The Final Hour

So, what *exactly* is net worth? What comes to mind when you think of the phrase? For some of us, we tend to go straight to our bank accounts and look at all the weekly, bi-weekly, or monthly income deposits. Others may think of corporate guys in suits who own yachts and speak confidently while laughing loudly using words referring to their' stock options' and 'brokerage accounts.' At first, I'll be all the way real. I certainly felt that way. Some of you may shrug without a clue and sigh, "Well, you tell me what net worth means."

Net worth is the value of all assets minus all liabilities at any given point in time. As previously shared, you have both appreciating and depreciating assets. Let me pause here quickly. Please note, we should easily rattle off terms like assets, personal balance sheets, and stock portfolios as casually as we say checking, savings, and paycheck. These terms should not be ascribed or associated only with specific demographics.

These financial terms can and should also be embraced in the black community just as we easily adopt phrases like "on fleek' into our everyday conversations.

These financial tools must be embraced as melanin terms and integrated more commonly into how we discuss our financial resources. Practice it in your next conversation. When someone asks you what you did over the weekend. Respond, "I updated my personal balance sheet." But *actually* do it that weekend prior, lol!

With that said, let's push forward. Your salary and bank account balances may comprise certain aspects of your overall wealth picture regarding your net worth. Yet those things alone are not the only factors in calculating your individual net worth. In fact, many very wealthy individuals receive a modest salary. For example, it was reported that Larry Page earned $1 a year from his work at Google, yet he had many more assets. Elon Musk of Tesla reportedly earned $37,000 a year, and Warren Buffett had a salary of $100,000 a year. All of these individuals are billionaires.

These examples show that it's income *and* assets that can provide an abundant financial picture. **So, why should we limit ourselves in thinking of wealth and finance just in terms of income?** For the most part, we have been distracted by the wrong numbers. We have to learn the critical difference between focusing on one's income versus one's net worth. Let's take a look at the current situation.

According to the Economic Policy Institute, the average net worth for black Americans is $95,261, compared to the average of $678,737 of white Americans. Does that statistic help to illuminate the importance that we start to focus more consistently on net worth? Absolutely!

If we want a shot at closing the wealth gap between black and white Americans, increasing our net worth has to be the goal—not just our salaries. The fight for a higher net worth must come at least partly from our refusal to be left behind when it comes to building wealth.

You know the joke where someone taps you on your right shoulder, you look right, while they do something mischievous to your left. That is an excellent analogy of what our focus on income and salary alone does. It distracts and keeps us turned away from the true measuring stick for wealth and financial success of net worth. So let's get our focus to the right place.

Examining the Numbers

Net Worth = Assets - Liabilities

So, how should we address these matters? We must examine the numbers up close. Don't get me wrong—reaching and achieving a high five, six, or even seven-figure income is an amazing accomplishment! At that level, many of us may feel a huge sense of accomplishment. Especially if those income levels are rarely achieved amongst your family and friends.

I was a very happy camper the first time my annual salary crossed that 6-figure threshold. **Yet all the zeros listed for your salary will not automatically outweigh your liabilities.** That's why you have to look at the full equation—lining up your assets next to your liabilities and doing the math. You must become an active participant in converting your income into growth-producing assets that can help catapult you into positive net worth.

Let's take a closer look at one of the core tenants of an average person's net worth and one of the best-known growth-producing assets—retirement investment accounts. A recent study listed by the Center of American Progress found that black Americans have, on average, $19,049 in liquid retirement savings, compared to $130,472 for white Americans. *That is an over $100k difference in just one asset alone*! No wonder this is a challenge. It further drives the importance of examining "our progress" from an overall net worth perspective and not just the outward displays culturally expected to accompany financial "success."

We must proactively create a space at our tables for sustainable wealth. By building habits of investing in *appreciating* assets and watching their worth multiply over the years, we can increase our collective wealth. When it comes to net worth, what matters most is how much you are keeping and growing. Yes, the higher your income, the greater resources you may have to increase your net worth. But don't get it twisted—a person in their mid-fifties can have a low salary, yet their net worth can be through the roof because of all the assets they have developed over the years.

Now that we have delved into the discussion on net worth's importance, how will you focus on your own personal numbers? Will you now give more consid-eration to appreciating assets that expand your net worth? Will you develop new financial management skills?

We all have to stretch and grow to get to new levels of wealth. Before we level up, though, let's take a moment to calculate your net worth as of today.

Let me note that you definitely should not get discouraged if you start with a negative number. That was actually our starting point not too long ago. However, with discipline and an intentional plan supported by the right habits and mindset, you can achieve a positive net worth.

My aim is to put you on the path to become an HNWI—an acronym for High Net Worth Individual. While this book is titled #7-Figure Net Worth, you may decide that your personal goal may be to achieve a 5- or 6-figure net worth. I applaud that, as well. Thoughtfully set your personal net worth goal and then work your ways toward it. Let's get you onto the path of achieving a high net worth of your own definition! Now, let's use this next worksheet to take a look at your current net worth.

Your Numbers

Calculating Your Personal Net Worth

· ·

In the previous two worksheets, you calculated the value of all of your current assets and then all of your current liabilities. To calculate your net worth, simply subtract the total of your assets from the total of your liabilities.

_____ − _____ = _____

    Assets   Liabilities   Net Worth

CHAPTER FOUR

Your Numbers
Household Income

> "Becoming disciplined with your thoughts and actions is more important than the actual money that you have coming into your household. Without that discipline, the money will leave more quickly than it came. That is one of the biggest mistakes people make when it comes to accumulating wealth."
>
> – Keith Willis, Founder, TheHoodieMillionaire.com

The most common place to start as it relates to finances is often monthly household income. Monthly household income is the total amount that you receive each month from all of your income sources. It can come from business, jobs, investments, alimony, child support, federal or state assistance, or another source. The total of all cash, physical checks, cash transfer applications, and direct deposits received within a month equals your monthly household income.

For many of us, monthly household income is the plumb line—or our very first measuring stick we assign to our financial lives. Unfortunately, this area needs immediate attention for many of us. Income and wages earned are among the fiercest battlegrounds for modern black Americans. Systematic wage inequality significantly contributes to the existing wealth gap.

The Economic Policy Institute confirms that the wage gap has continued to grow between black and white Americans since 2000. No matter how you slice it, a significant black–white wage gap still emerges across various education levels. Even when considering black workers with advanced degrees plus work experience, there remains a considerable wage gap compared to our white counterparts.

As economists control factors such as age, gender, education, and region, black workers are paid 14.9% less than white workers. To break that down, if a white person made $100,000, the black person would make $85,100. If neither receives a raise, and all things remain equal, the white person would have made $1,000,000 in ten years, while the black person would make $851,000. What a difference! We haven't even talked about the difference that $149K would do if invested during that period!

A key strategy for modern black Americans to overcome systematic wage bias is through black entrepreneurship and creating multiple income streams. In the **Habits** section, we will discuss various income streams in greater detail. Phrases that we often hear, such as "last hired first fired," reinforce the reality that many black Americans cannot merely rely on 'steady jobs.' Instead, many of us must also find additional income sources if we intend to build wealth at similar rates as other Americans.

Thankfully, there are also ongoing policy initiatives being put forth to help eradicate systematic discrimination. For example, "baby bonds" that have been advocated by black economists William Darity Jr. *and* Darrick Hamilton are being proposed as legislation by Senator Cory Booker. We must match these macro-level initiatives with wise daily micro-actions.

On average, we have less capital to work with, so we must be *even more* careful with every dollar we spend. Like the scene in the TV show, Scandal, where Rowan Pope (a black father played by Joe Morton) speaking to his adult daughter Olivia Pope (played by Kerry Washington) tells her to repeat the family mantra that many of us have also heard since birth. Pope dutifully recites, "You have to be twice as good to get half as much."

This mantra often applies to the budgetary and investment decisions we make. Fair or unfair, the bottom line is we have to put in that work! Our monthly income demands our full attention! Every single dollar of income entrusted in our hands remains one of the most powerful tools that many of us will ever have to attain financial health, build high-value net worth, and create a family fortune that could last generations.

For now, let's check out the current state of affairs and detail—undeniably one of the most important numbers in our financial portfolio—your monthly income. We can daydream about, strategize, and plot for all the immense financial possibilities a bit later.

Your Numbers
Monthly Household Income

. . . .

PLEASE FILL IN THE NUMBER FOR EACH INCOME SOURCE BELOW

ACTIVE INCOME

JOB				
BUSINESSES				
OTHER				

TOTAL ACTIVE INCOME

PASSIVE INCOME

BUSINESS				
ALIMONY / CHILD SUPPORT				
REAL ESTATE				
DIVIDENDS				
PROFIT SHARE PAYMENTS				
OTHER				

TOTAL PASSIVE INCOME

_____ + _____ = _____
Monthly Active Income   Monthly Passive Income   Total Monthly Income

CHAPTER FIVE

Your Numbers
Paycheck Deductions

> *"Everybody hates math until their paycheck shows up a little funny."*
>
> *– So many social media posts*

We often start financial plans and monthly budgets looking at the amount of our take-home pay—the amount shows up as direct deposits or on checks. Your take-home pay—also known as your net income—is often a solid place to start. Yet, I have learned to take it one step further.

Examine Your Withholdings

For a more accurate financial picture, start with your gross pay rather than your take-home pay. Your gross pay—also known as your gross income— is the amount received *before* any taxes, medical insurance, retirement contributions, or other withholdings are taken out of your paycheck.

Each withholding line item on your paycheck stub needs your attention. Your withholdings represent potential working capital that can provide you with essential dollars and cents to help you reach your financial objectives. So as we look at your monthly household income, let's dig one step deeper and look at all of your withholdings with the next worksheet.

Take Action!

After writing each withholding amount, examine the current amount and coverage needed for each line item for the Employer Benefits worksheet. Work with your human resources (HR) department, or use financial software to adjust any amounts that are too high or too low for your current needs.

Bragging Rights

Once you complete this step, we want to hear about it! Share what you learned or what you changed in the #7-Figure Net Worth Facebook group.

Your Numbers
Paycheck Deductions

· ·

Let's take an up-close and personal look at your paycheck stub. Write each of the deduction amounts from your paycheck into the Paycheck Deductions worksheet.

Study each amount attentively. Realize that each item represents **your money** which you have the opportunity to steward, preserve, and dispense.

DEDUCTIONS

FEDERAL TAXES	_____
STATE TAXES	_____
CITY / LOCAL TAXES	_____
SOCIAL SECURITY (6.2% OF GROSS INCOME)	_____
MEDICARE / FICA (1.45% OF GROSS INCOME)	_____
MEDICAL INSURANCE	_____
HEALTH SAVINGS ACCOUNT	_____
FLEXIBLE SPENDING ACCOUNT	_____
EYE CARE	_____
DENTAL PLAN	_____
401K / RETIREMENT	_____
OTHER	_____
OTHER	_____

GROSS INCOME PER PAYCHECK

$ _____

TOTAL DEDUCTIONS

$ _____

NET INCOME AFTER WITHHOLDINGS

$ _____

Let me just say it! A big refund check is *not* the goal—y'all!

Actually, the goal is to receive a very minimal tax fund each year—as close to zero as possible. I know that tax refund may be what you use each year for that big splurge, a much-needed trip, or to knock out a chunk of debt. However, you should have that money—**your money**—in your hands much earlier than that. Properly adjusting the amount of taxes that you pay allows you to have full control of where you allocate your dollars throughout the year. Instead of loaning it interest free for Unc Sam to give it back to you on his own schedule.

Some of y'all may not want to hear me on this. No problem! At least you cannot say no one ever told you. For those that want access to every dollar so you can make it grow, here are a couple of ways you can adjust the refund amount you receive each year.

If you are employed, it all starts with your W-4 or the employee's withholding certificate that your employer has on file. The W-4 form includes details like your filing status, amount of credits and other incomes, deduction amount, and any additional amount to withhold from your pay. The form helps your employer determine how much to deduct from your paycheck.

If you are self-employed, you will want to discuss adjusting your quarterly tax payment amounts and insuring you have a tax advantaged investment plan in place to lower your overall tax burden.

By using the tax estimator on the IRS website, you can adjust your withholdings, allowances, or quarterly tax payments so that you end up owing as close to zero at year-end as possible.

You can also compare your taxes from one year to the next. For this, compare your income tax returns for each year—you can find it on your 2019's return on line 16 of your Form-1040, 2018's return on line 15, and so on.

Now compare your income for each year and find if your tax has increased with any increases in your income. After reviewing, discuss with your tax advisor ways to lower taxable income in the future. Perhaps, by raising 401(k) plan contributions or putting money into flexible spending accounts or health savings accounts.

Got it? Ready, set, aim for zero!

CHAPTER SIX

Your Numbers
Employer Benefits

> *"Opportunity is everywhere. The key is to develop the vision to see it."*
>
> *– Anonymous*

In many books about success and wealth that I've read, there is often a sentence or two about the importance of seeing an opportunity and taking advantage of it. While we are in adulting mode, let's take a peek at some often–overlooked employer benefits that could be instrumental to your HNWI journey. If you are going to secure the bag, you cannot afford to leave any benefits on the table!

Look at each benefit below and identify the ones that your employer provides that may benefit you now. If you are self–employed or run a business with employees, think about additional ways to help your employees to reach their financial goals.

Employee Assistance Program (EAP)

Complimentary counseling sessions offered through EAP programs are one of the most overlooked gems in the workplace. As we discussed, positive mental health is key to your financial success—because, without good mental health, it is difficult to function while working. If your employer offers EAP sessions as a part of your benefits package, please consider taking advantage of the counseling benefits. A free counseling session may be offered to support your transition through a personally tough phase, to help you grow professionally, or even just provide an overall mental health check-in.

Legal Plan

Having even a basic will in place can save your family from years of hardships. Even handwritten ones are only legally viable if completed in the presence of two witnesses, preferably notarized. Without a will, your estate, including all your money, property, possessions, etc. will more than likely be subject to intestacy laws—and may create hard feelings for and amongst those left behind. Intestacy laws are where your state of residence determines how the property is distributed. It can lead to your hard-earned assets being tied up in probate court as the state appoints someone to handle your estate—often a family member. Even if the person appointed has management skills and is okay with doing this—there are added issues. For example, between court fees and unpaid creditors, the person's time, money, and resources may dwindle as they attempt to clarify what you could have written beforehand.

Y'all know the drama that can happen amongst our people just during the course of a regular funeral weekend. We don't need to add any additional cause for drama or controversy. Investigate your current benefits through your employer, as some companies or agencies offer a legal plan to cover the cost of creating a basic will. My husband and I completed ours with a local attorney specializing in this area through his work plan without paying anything additional.

If it is not offered, you should likely explore hiring an attorney on your own to create one. There are other options besides wills. These may include (but not excluded to) living trusts, joint ownership, or even beneficiary designations. Creating a legally viable plan for transferring your assets is something you should definitely check off your financial adulting checklist.

Tuition Reimbursement Program

Invest in your genius! Seriously! After years of seeing my "could-have-otherwise-been-investment" capital disappear to student loan payments, I now view tuition reimbursement programs as something that *must be* utilized. Otherwise, you may be once again leaving money on the table. Both in increased earning opportunities and the money you may otherwise opt to spend from your personal banking account on professional development. Take a moment right now to think about if you can complete a training program, a professional certificate, or a viable degree that will increase your marketability and earning power. Check out your employer's requirements. Some employers are even willing to cover a portion or all of the costs depending upon the connection between the degree program and the employee's work. It's a benefit definitely worth exploring.

Any Other Great Benefits?

Whether it is vacation days, an EAP counselor, pet insurance, or complimentary legal sessions for a will, review all benefits your employer currently offers. Then, identify the ones you can utilize. Make a list of these benefits and highlight any action you may need to take to participate. Schedule time to speak with knowledgeable sources (i.e., lawyers, EAP counselors, HR representatives) in order to maximize the return you can realize from your benefits.

Your Numbers
Employer Benefits

· ·

1. Are you able to access your benefits package either in paper or electronic format?

2. Are any of the aforementioned benefits offered through your employer?

3. If yes, which of these benefits or others offered can benefit you on your #7-Figure Net Worth journey?

4. Please write down which benefits you plan to take advantage of, who you need to contact, their contact information, and the date you will contact them by.

CHAPTER SEVEN

Your Numbers
Insurance Coverage

> *"Failing to prepare is preparing to fail."*
>
> – *Coach John Wooden*

My husband has coached basketball for many years, so after a decade of marriage, I have found myself thinking of many items from a sports-related context. Early in your financial journey, many of the steps you need to take concerning insurance are defensive measures. You want to protect yourself against the financial impact of a fire with home insurance, a car crash with auto insurance, a major trip to the hospital with medical insurance, or even an untimely passing of a loved one with life insurance.

As your income, assets, and overall net worth grow, it becomes more important to have defensive *and* offensive insurance strategies. As our financial picture evolved, one of our first offensive steps was to investigate how a carefully designed cash value policy could provide self- or infinite banking for us. If you have not heard of infinite banking, it is definitely something you should read up on.

We began to evaluate our medical insurance differently and opt for plans with higher deductibles. We then added more to our health savings account (HSA), understanding the long-term tax and retirement benefits that can accumulate over time within these accounts. We studied the concept of being self-insured and began to develop an evolved view of insurance. We transitioned from viewing insurance as only a defensive tool to understanding that it can also be an offensive aspect of our financial strategy.

Regardless of the strategic role that insurance plays, it's essential to get a solid understanding of both what you have *and* what you need. So, let's start by talking about some of the most common types of insurance: car, renters or home, and life insurance.

Car Insurance

At the most standard level, if you have a car, you should have car insurance. In most states, it's required by law. Suffice it to say that attempting to save money by "riding dirty" is definitely not a wealth-building strategy. Why would you want to risk facing tremendous financial liability driving your vehicle with no insurance? Chamillionaire may have had success with the song, but it won't work out that way for you. Trust me!

Sure, you may be an excellent driver, but that doesn't account for the plethora of reckless drivers that can cause you to unintentionally run into another vehicle. No matter what, at that point, you are at fault. If you don't have insurance, you can expect whatever financial plans you had to come to a sudden halt—and possibly go in reverse.

Ensuring that you have car insurance and sufficient coverage levels is a core part of financial responsibility. Do you have other vehicles such as boats, RVs, or motorcycles? You will want to ensure you have adequate insurance coverage for those as well.

Renters/Home Insurance

Not all people add this level of protection, but it is a wise move to do so. Renters insurance is for occupants who do not own the property but want to protect their personal belongings in a flood, fire, or other natural disasters. Homeowners insurance covers the home in the same situations. However, if you are renting the place, the homeowner's insurance only covers the house, not the tenant's belongings.

If you have not explored getting a policy to cover your home or belongings in your rental, ensure that you do so. This is a core defensive strategy that you want to have to protect your finances in case of the unexpected.

Umbrella Policies

Umbrella insurance is a personal liability policy that provides coverage in excess of other policies you may hold, such as homeowner and vehicle. I consider this policy type in the category of offensive strategies. These policies provide coverage for others that are impacted in incidents, including bodily injury or possession damage. It can also offer insurance for other types of losses not covered by other policies. As your net worth grows, you will want to seriously consider adding an umbrella type of policy to your portfolio. You do not want an unexpected event to create the risk of your hard-earned assets being subject to a lawsuit or claim.

Life Insurance

Now, I know we all think we will live forever once we make it to Wakanda, but we have to be realistic while still here in America. As you are in the early stages of your career and your journey to financial freedom, you will want to ensure that you have a life insurance policy in place. Life insurance is necessary; no matter your age, you want to prepare yourself for the end of your life here. Eventually, as you increase your net worth, you may get to a place that you and your financial advisory squad determine that you can become self-insured. In the meantime, you will want to work with an insurance advisor or an insurance company to determine the type of insurance and the type of policies that work best for your individual situation.

Types of Life Insurance

There are two major types of life insurance—term and whole life. Term insurance is the simplest form of life insurance. It only pays if death occurs during the policy term, usually from one to 30 years. There are two basic types of term life insurance policies: level term and decreasing term. Insurance Information Institute defines the level term as policies where the death benefit stays the same throughout the policy and a decreasing term as policies where the death benefit drops, usually in one-year increments throughout the policy.

Whole life or permanent insurance pays a death benefit whenever you die—even if you actually make it to Wakanda one day, and you live to 200 years old. Now, that is unlikely, but it basically covers you for the rest of your life. There are also branches underneath whole/permanent life—traditional whole life, universal life, and variable universal life. Most insurance companies say that a reasonable amount for life insurance is six to 10 times the amount of your annual salary.

As your financial journey progresses, there will be additional ways cash value policies can become a part of your wealth accumulation strategy.

Critical Illness + Disability Insurance

In the infamous words of Forrest Gump, "Life is like a box of chocolate. You never know what you are going to get." Life happens. The unfortunate reality is that you may get sick or injured in a manner that impairs your ability to work the way you are used to. Sadly, in situations like that, we can't just Thanos snap our bills away. Yes, they will still come, and after you've repaired your credit, I'm sure you don't want it tumbling back downhill. If you find yourself in that situation, you don't want to be forced to have to tap into your savings or liquidate investments. So, if you are reading this right now, it is for a good reason. It is a good idea to make preparations for "just in case" situations that could occur later in life. It is better to be prepared and not need it than to be unprepared and not have it.

Critical Illness

When you have an illness that requires extensive medical treatment and changes your quality of life, this type of insurance covers high medical costs for hospital visits and surgeries. Critical illness insurance policies can provide additional coverage beyond what is covered by your medical insurance. It is a great plan to keep you from needing to tap into your savings or leaning on something else while you focus on restoring your health.

Short-Term or Long-Term Disability

Disability insurance benefits those eligible for full or partial loss of wages due to a non-work-related injury, illness, or accident. For employers that offer this benefit, most pay the full coverage amount. If your employer doesn't offer this coverage, you will want to look into obtaining a policy on your own.

In addition to these above-listed types of insurance, business owners will want to consider adding these policies as well.

Key Person Insurance

In many cases, you are the light that shines bright in your business and keeps all the trains on track. As an entrepreneur, it is an offensive strategy to ensure that your business is protected if the owner or other significant employee passes away. This is a life insurance policy where your company serves as the beneficiary and will be responsible for making the premium payments. This is also sometimes referred to as business life insurance.

General Liability Insurance

You invest a lot of time and hustle to see your business become a success. You want to ensure that your efforts and profits have adequate protection. General liability policies help to protect your business in the circumstance that someone sues you for causing damage to property or bodily injury. In certain types of businesses, an insurance advisor may also recommend adding a professional liability policy covering errors, omissions, or professional mistakes.

Whether focused on just your defense or both your defensive and offensive strategies, it is vital to gain a solid understanding of all the insurance policies you have and may need. In this next worksheet, we will take a look at your current insurance landscape.

Did You Know?

In the 1920s, black families were systematically denied coverage by insurance companies. As early as 1787, African Americans gave a resilient response because home and life insurance policies were not available. Local neighborhoods organized bereavement societies that allowed people to pay into an administered pool of money.

A member would make consistent payments into this pool. Upon passing, the bereavement society would provide burial in nice attire and a celebratory funeral program. Many funeral traditions that are part of modern-day black culture are rooted in the grand fashion of burial provided by these self-administered bereavement societies.

Your Numbers
Insurance Coverage

For this worksheet, let's take a look at your insurance profile. It is vital to identify insurance types, and the coverage amounts you need to ensure adequate financial protection.

While on your journey to achieving a #7–Figure Net Worth, it is also vital that you identify the insurance strategies that you will need to reach your goals.

KEY INSURANCE TERMS TO KNOW

- Deductible
- Premium
- Co-Pay
- Beneficiary
- Provider Network

- Claims Adjustment Expenses
- Accumulation Period
- Provider Network
- Annuity

- Commencement Date
- Date of Issue
- Blanket Coverage

There are more than forty (40+) key insurance terms pivotal to your understanding of insurance coverage. For example, the National Association of Insurance Commissioners provide an accessible Glossary at https://content.naic.org/consumer_glossary.htm that may prove useful. Before signing any insurance documents, take a moment to look up any terms you see or need to understand. Your applied knowledge will provide the power you need to support yourself and your family.

	PROVIDER	COVERAGE AMOUNT	MONTHLY PAYMENT
MEDICAL			
AUTO			
HOME			
SHORT TERM DISABILITY			
TERM LIFE INSURANCE			
PET			

7-Figure Net Worth

Once you have armed yourself with core insurance coverage, move forward in building enduring wealth of a lasting intergenerational impact. Consider, for instance, exploring options and augmenting your core coverage. You can do so with additional types of insurance. Take the time to understand insurance products of your choice. Determine which are good for you.

	Understand It? Y / N	Have It? Y / N	Need It? Y / N
General Liability Umbrella			
Key Person Insurance (Business Owners)			
Annuity			
Cash Value Life Insurance			
Cash Value Life Insurance (For Infinite Banking)			

For each insurance policy that you have, review the terms. Highlight any concepts that you do not understand. Call each provider or agent and spend 15 minutes to an hour talking through each element until you have a solid understanding of the offered product.

#BLACK *Millennial* **ADULTING**

Budget Impact

As part of *The Budgetnista's* Live Richer Challenge, participants are encouraged to look at all insurance policies and contact competitors for new quotes. Once you have these quotes in hand, you can provide that competitive quote to your current provider or decide to move to the new company (provided that they still offer you the full range of coverage needed). Again, we have to account for every potential dollar that we can use to build wealth.

When discussing this approach, Tiffany Aliche shares a key point. Be mindful that if insurance companies ask for your social security number when gaining quotes—this may trigger an inquiry on your credit report. I strongly encourage you to first research how insurance-related inquiries may impact your credit report and score. If you are in a position to tolerate those potential inquiries, get out a sheet of paper for notes, and give some competitors to your current insurance providers a ring. As in most things in life and business, having leverage can place you in a better position. Arm yourself with the leverage you need to save money!

Medical Insurance

> *"Do the best you can until you know better. Then when you know better, do better."*
>
> – Maya Angelou

L et's chat about how you can strategically choose your medical insurance plan – beginning with a throwback look at how I used to do it. Alexa, play Back in the Day by Ahmad. "Back in the days when I was young I'm not a kid anymore..." When I was just entering the workforce in my early 20s, I would wait until the *very last* day of open enrollment. After hastily picking a plan, I would often go with the cheapest monthly deductible. I naively equated the 'cheapest' with 'best.'

Later in life—after giving birth to two beautiful children—I saw the huge financial difference that a specific medical insurance plan can have on your finances. Let me be completely transparent—during my first pregnancy, I had some "really good benefits." When I gave birth to my first daughter, given her health complications and the time she needed in the intensive care unit, we came home with a hospital bill of $200K+. Whoa! My eyes bulged when I saw that bill. However, I did a little dance when I saw the portion of the bill that was our responsibility—hospital co-pays of $200 for each of us—$400 total!

Three years later, while embracing life as an entrepreneur, we were on my hubby's insurance. Thankfully my second daughter was full-term and healthy. After her birth, we were sent a hospital bill of about $30K, much lower than before. But this time, we were responsible for about $5K. What was the difference? Keep in mind that we are comparing a payment of $400 on a $200K bill versus $5,000 on a bill of only $30K. The difference was participating in a *different* type of medical plan the second time around.

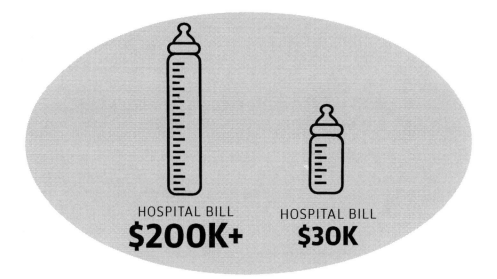

HOSPITAL BILL
$200K+

HOSPITAL BILL
$30K

While there are similarities in these scenarios, many things, including the insurance company and the employer, were different. Yet for most of us—the difference between the $25 a month plan and the $150 a month plan could have major financial implications if a major medical event were to take place. Understanding your current health situation and choosing your plan accordingly could be the difference of a medical bill with your personal financial responsibility equating to the cost of a weekend getaway versus the cost of a car.

Through these up close and personal scenarios, we became more intentional about planning our medical insurance. So again, we apply the offensive versus defensive paradigm here. We must start to take an offensive position and be aware of the variations between insurance plans. For example, are you aware of how "fee for service" differs from "health insurance on a retainer"? Do you know the difference between a health maintenance organization (HMOs) and a preferred provider organization (PPOs)? You must not shy away from educating yourself on these ideas so that you can pick the medical insurance coverage that is the very best for you and your family.

Why is this so important?

The types of medical insurance you select can have a *huge* impact on your finances. One of the top forms of debt that many Americans face is medical bills. Due to bias in the healthcare system and systematic discrimination often impacting nutrition, black Americans bear a disproportionate amount of that debt. For example, African Americans had 2.6 times higher odds of medical debt than white Americans, according to the National Institutes of Health. Urban food deserts and some of our *ahem* cultural norms around eating habits (i.e., grandma's greens perfectly seasoned with fatback) also contribute to nutritional deficits that can often lead to higher levels of infection and disease within our communities (i.e., grandma's sugar and high blood pressure).

We can choose to be proactive in reducing the chance that we will incur medical-related debt. Whether your medical insurance is through your employer or purchased on the open market, it is essential to understand how each factor of your plan impacts your ability to choose your medical care. The burden of facing unexpected costs associated with any required medical care—whether through your primary care doctor, or your specialist, your dentist, or your eye doctor—can be potentially avoided with a little upfront research and legwork.

Please don't be like my younger self and wait until the last minute to review your medical plan options. Educate yourself now on the nuance of each term and plan. That 800-number listed on your medical plan—pick up the phone and call it. Talk to the medical insurance plan provider—ask them lots of questions. Don't be intimidated. Get educated. Know better. Do better.

Melanin Millionaire Tip

Protect Your Health

> *"If you have your health, you're wealthy."*
>
> – Frank Coleman,
> my beloved godfather

The most important asset you will ever have is your physical health. This sometimes-overlooked key to building wealth ensures that you eat healthy, exercise, drink water, get adequate sleep, and take vitamins. Do whatever it takes to address your physical and medical challenges. My god-father used to always tell me in his hearty booming voice, "If you have your health, you're wealthy." That is true in more ways than one. Good health in and of itself is a form of wealth. It is also a key factor in your ability to generate financial wealth. Begin to see health decisions as financial ones—in the sense that when you feel better, the more energy you can exert towards achieving your financial goals.

For example, when I work intensely and diligently on one of my projects, I've been known to completely cut out meat for a finite period. I need to preserve all my physical energy for my work—not merely on digesting food! The state of my phys-ical body does more than impact my ability to complete assignments. It helps me to think clearly, leverage ideas, and seize opportunities tied to greater production.

Guard Your Mental

Physical health can also impact mental health. For example, the Canadi-an Mental Health Association (CMHA) confirms this reality in giving the World Health Organization's findings. CMHA stated that "[folks] with chronic physical conditions are at risk of developing poor mental health." While this may have an impact, the opposite is also true—mental health impacts physical health.

For instance, in a Harvard Study, those who were optimistic had nearly a 50% less risk of an initial cardiovascular event. *Translation: Being happy makes your heart happy!* Considering the evidence presented, we need the soundness of body and mind to be fully engaged. Our lives—not just our financial lives—depend upon it!

Y'all already know this is critically important for the modern black American. Many black folks have struggled against ailments that I previously mentioned, such as hypertension (high blood pressure) and Type II diabetes (sugar). So we must be especially aware of how we can integrate health care strategies for greater wellness levels. Give yourself a leg up using the knowledge to make lifestyle changes that will allow you to build the life you desire. Even when issues arise or disease crops up, you must know early to address the matter. So do whatever is necessary to invest in your top asset—you!

Know Your Worth

You are worth so much more than the money you make or the assets you own. Which brings me to my next question: what will it take for *you* to embrace *optimal* health? If you are currently in poor health, that may mean first moving from poor to good to great to optimal. Optimal health—physically, mentally, emotionally, and spiritually is that zone where you wake up energized, perform better, are positive, and you can expand your capacity to execute in ways that can reap abundant rewards. So what changes in your eating habits, personal routine, and decision-making can help you get to a place of optimal health?

One of the most straightforward strategies for achieving and maintaining excellent physical health is simply getting an annual health physical! In many cases, you can do this at no additional cost with most medical insurance plans. Yet many people will not schedule this yearly appointment. Don't be that person. Whether it is anxiety or something else—push past the fear and learn what you need to make the necessary changes for a healthier, peaceful, and successful life.

Finally, I want you to consider the ideas presented and answer the questions in the following worksheet. No worries if you don't know at first —these questions are also action steps to guide you to move toward a healthier you. Let's get it!

Melanin Millionaire Tip
Protect Your Health

. . . .

1. What is the name of your primary care doctor?

2. When was the date of your last wellness check-up?

If it has been more than two years, please schedule an appointment with your primary care doctor in the next two (2) weeks. If you do not have one—that's okay because you can reach out to your medical insurance provider, who can give guidance and a list in choosing one. Again, if you do not have this exact date, please contact your doctor. Make an appointment and then add it to your calendar.

3. When will you have your next annual physical?

4. What fees are associated with you getting an annual physical with your current medical insurance plan? If you are unsure, find out by calling your physician or your medical insurance company.

5. Do you have a wellness maintenance line in your monthly budget? If feasible, consider adding a wellness line item to your monthly budget for healthy 'extras' like gym/yoga memberships, massages, vitamins, protein shakes, or healthy snacks.

While you may feel some initial apprehension, our goal is to see you healthy, wealthy, and wise. Do not delay your annual health visits—schedule now—your health is invaluable! By making wellness a priority, the rest will follow.

Health Savings Accounts (HSAs)

L everaging health savings accounts (HSAs) as a financial asset is also a key concept to understand. A health savings account (HSA) is a pre-tax account that you can contribute to and use for approved medical expenses. Unlike a flexible spending account (FSA), the scope of what can be used on a health savings account (HSA) is typically narrower than a flexible spending account (FSA). When understood and leveraged correctly, it can become a powerful tool for a couple of reasons. One is the tax advantage. The second being retirement. Here's why? If you pick a medical insurance plan with a higher monthly premium and a lower deductible amount, the higher premium may provide peace of mind, but you may pay unnecessary costs.

Let me explain. In the first scenario, let's say your monthly premium is $150 per month. You end up only going to the doctor for your annual physical and again for another visit. The second visit triggers a $20 co-pay. You will not have saved much. You have spent $1,800 in medical premiums at the end of the year, and you will never see those funds again.

For the second scenario, let's say you are in pretty good health—and you choose a plan with a lower premium like $40 per month. This means you have an extra $110 per month. Instead of paying that extra $110 to an insurance premium like the first scenario, you choose to instead invest those funds into an HSA account. This results in $1,320 annually in your HSA that can be used for any anticipated out of pocket exams, including your annual physical and other medical visits. Those funds stay with you until you decide to use them. Now, let us apply the same two doctor visits to the second scenario.

Like the first scenario, you have an annual physical and one additional visit that year. In this case, however, you are required to make a co-insurance payment of $200 for the second visit. This is ten times higher than the $20 co-pay in the first scenario. Yet thankfully, you pay the fee with your HSA card. At the end of the year, you now have an additional $1,120 in funds that you can invest, which grows year after year. **Contrast this $1,120 of money invested in your HSA account with the medical premiums of $1,800 that you paid to the insurance company.** By taking a different approach to your medical insurance plan and leveraging HSAs, you have now gained more than $1,000, which will only yield greater and can carry over for medical expenses during retirement.

In short, the benefits of HSAs can be summarized in the following ways:

Save. Start the HSA with automatic deduction and take care of your co-pays for your higher deductible plans using your HSA card. *Are you thinking of additional medical expenses like your child's braces or your spouse's reading glasses?* HSA can be a great way to take care of those matters as well!

Invest. Your HSAs accounts are a wellness investment. Yet it has been used in other ways. For instance, a portion may be invested in securities once reaching certain account balances, including mutual funds.

Contribute. You're in the driver's seat! Once opened, the HSA account is yours. Review your monthly budget and during open enrollment—set aside a healthy amount. If you are working full-time, try taking $100 a month from eating out— and add it to your HSA account. Remember, healthy savings grow—unwise spending diminishes.

Manage. Does your employer offer a matching percentage based on your contribution? Accept the challenge. Manage your growth by raising your percentage. Maximize the opportunity to increase. Even if you change jobs, you can transfer your HSA accounts.

Grow Beyond a Year. If your HSA account is open, your added money is steadily scoring points for you as any remaining funds roll over into the next year.

Expect Tax–Free Funds Irrespective of Income Level. As HSAs grow tax-free—you may be surprised to know there are currently no income limits on these accounts (*as in the case of Roth IRAs—we will discuss later*). Regardless of how little or how much money you make, you can increase your fund investment through HSAs. However, there are maximum yearly contribution limits. The IRS has announced that 2021 contribution limits will be $3,600 for individuals and $7,200 for families – excluding catch up exceptions.

Embrace Health & Use HSAs for Your Purposes during Retirement. While you can utilize the funds for eligible tax–free health–related causes right now—one thing changes upon the age of 65. After 65, you may use HSAs for other reasons without penalty.

Now, for the most part, the scenarios I explained may not apply if you anticipate significant medical expenses each year. If you have a condition requiring frequent medical attention, it may still be worthwhile to look at your current medical plans and HSA options. Create a couple of different scenarios to compare your choices.

After comparing your viable options, identify the most financially beneficial combination. Choose the one that will minimize your after–tax out of pocket expenses and limit your exposure to a financially debilitating event.

Now, let's look at your medical–related spending and evaluate what, if any, changes you should make to gain the highest financial advantage.

Your Numbers
Insurance Coverage

Medical Insurance and HSAs

	YEAR TO DATE	LAST YEAR
MONTHLY PREMIUM PAID BY YOU		
MONTHLY PREMIUM PAID CONTRIBUTED BY EMPLOYER *(IF APPLICABLE)*		
TOTAL OUT OF POCKET SPENT ON PREMIUMS		
INDIVIDUAL DEDUCTIBLE		
FAMILY DEDUCTIBLE *(IF APPLICABLE)*		
# OF SPECIALIST VISIT		
# OF PRIMARY CARE VISITS		
TOTAL AMOUNT BILLED FOR YOUR CARE		
TOTAL AMOUNT SPENT OUT OF POCKET FOR YOUR CARE		

Is there a plan with a lower monthly premium that can fit your healthcare needs?

Once the amount is lowered, given your wellness level, would it make sense to invest the savings generated from the difference between your old and new premium amounts?

Could you invest the savings into a newly created HSA account? For example, let's say your monthly premium was $275. You change your policy. Now it is $175. Could you invest the difference of $100 into an HSA account?

When does the open enrollment period take place for your employer?

During that period, are you able to make the necessary changes to your health care plan with ease and knowledge?

If so, have you added the dates to your calendar to respond accordingly? If not, who will you need to contact to make this happen?

CHAPTER EIGHT

Your Numbers
Credit Scores

> *"You should give that to me just off GP alone."*
>
> – Black folks in America

"You *should give that to me just off GP alone."* I know I'm not the only person that has heard that phrase at different times in my life. In the black community, GP (or General Purpose) is what we say to get something based on "credit." Not credit in how the financial world uses the word, but in a way that says, "I'll pay you back later." Although we understand the term in the everyday sense, the concept also transitions into the financial world. It is the same principle, except one is in a white tee and the other in a business suit.

That Dude FICO

While GP is the "white tee" version of credit, a FICO credit score could be considered the "business suit" version. According to MyFico, a FICO score is defined as "a three-digit number based on the information in your credit reports. It helps lenders determine how likely you are to repay a loan."

Lenders use this number and associated information to establish how likely you are to repay or default on a loan. That score can impact how much you get approved to borrow, how many months you have to repay, and how much it will cost (the interest rate.) Those three numbers can impact everything from where you live and what you drive to getting a loan to start your business. There can be a direct correlation between your credit score and your quality of life in many cases.

Your credit rating is placed in one of five categories:

- Poor (below 580)
- Fair (580–669)
- Good (670–739)
- Very good (740–799)
- Excellent (above 800)

This isn't to say that people with fair credit scores can't get a reasonable interest rate on a loan because several factors go into deciding loan approval. While this scale provides commonly accepted guidelines, every lender uses their own criteria for what FICO scores they will accept. Lenders combine other information with the FICO score to determine what applicants will receive green light along with respective rates. So, it is possible to find yourself in a decent situation with fair credit. It is more likely, though, that you will find yourself with more favorable loan terms with good to exceptional credit scores.

The Bureaus

There are several different credit bureaus in the US Three are of major national significance: Equifax, Experian, and TransUnion. These bureaus are the most prominent for tracking, aggregating, and reporting information about consumers' credit-related behavior. While they are the three major credit reporting agencies, they don't always report the same information. This tidbit becomes extremely important if you find yourself in a situation where you desire to repair your credit and improve your scores.

During a rental application, mortgage, or another loan process, your lender may not check all three credit bureaus before approving or denying your application. Along the same lines, lenders may not report credit activity to all three credit bureaus—which means that your credit score could differ between the three agencies. That is the primary reason why you should grab your credit report from each bureau. A few charges on the report may not show up on another, so if you want to completely improve your credit, it's best to compare and contrast.

The Real

Even with an academic perspective in place, I'll go ahead and be honest to say I have mixed feelings about credit scores. There have been days where I felt like credit scores were financial X's, as Dave Ramsey would say. It still aggravates me to think of the years of on-time student loan payments that contributed to my credit score. Oh, how different my net worth would look today if I had invested all those payments instead. Those funds could *right now* be working actively in the stock market, yielding returns.

At the same time, I am graeful to have a 700+ credit score because I know what it took in my own personal journey to get there. Like I said . . . mixed feelings. Where I have landed for the moment on credit scores is much like my business philosophy — it is all about having viable options.

Where *you* land may depend on your personal financial philosophy and how you decide to strategically leverage debt in pursuit of your financial goals. Let me be clear—I am not talking about everyday consumer debt here— swiping credit cards and using student loan check refunds to purchase depreciating assets like cars and clothes. I am specifically discussing business debt that is thoughtfully leveraged to create and establish appreciating assets. In this way, you may find a high credit score useful in gaining access to necessary capital from traditional financial institutions.

You may be in the camp where you want to be off the grid. You no longer desire a credit score because you are debt-free and never want to use credit again. That is fine—I celebrate you! On the other hand, you may want to keep a great score, given your business goals. Accordingly, you may want strategic financing options available to assist you to achieve those goals. I understand and celebrate this too.

Like the diversity of our hair—curly, straight, kinky, locs, or bald—finance can also be very personal. The goal is to have viable and well thought out options from which to choose. As you craft your individual #7-Figure Net Worth blueprint, I recommend these steps:

1. Know your credit scores.

2. Understand which aspects of your financial journey you desire to leverage using the credit scores to increase your appreciating assets and achieve your business goals.

3. If your current credit scores are not what you desire, work on raising that score in alignment with your goals.

Improving Your Credit

If you are in the third category and find yourself with a poor or fair credit score, you may initially feel like you are in a frustrating uphill battle. The good news is that things are not always as hard as they may initially seem. I know firsthand—been there, done that. In this case, the key is equipping yourself with the knowledge and taking the necessary steps to improve your situation. While there is no "one size fits all" for repairing your credit, if you desire to improve your score, here are a few steps that I found helpful in raising my credit scores.

Disputing Charges

Credit bureaus are not always right, and it may not be from any fault of their own. Sometimes, lenders provide inaccurate information that negatively affects your credit. There have been cases of payments reported delinquent when the payment came in on time. Or maybe there is a charge impacting your credit that should have fallen off by now. For example, collection accounts are supposed to come off after seven years, while a chapter 7 bankruptcy can stay on for as long as ten. Find out the details of the debt and if there are inaccuracies, dispute them.

Pay off Debt

I know sometimes we don't want to pay if we don't absolutely have to, but "somebody look to your neighbor on your right and say, '**keep your word**.'" If there is a legit debt on your credit report, contact the lender to see if they are willing to settle. More times than not, even if the lender has sold the debt to a collection agency, they will settle for much less than you owe. Depending on the debt, paying it off can quickly catapult your credit score from one level to the next.

Be careful to negotiate a positive reporting of that settlement on your credit report as part of the agreement.

Limit Credit Usage/Keep a Credit Card with a Low Balance

The credit utilization ratio (CUR) is also a key factor when determining your credit score. To calculate this ratio, you will need to add all of your current credit card balances. Then divide that amount by your total credit limit on all your cards. For example, suppose you typically charge about $2,000 each month and your total credit limit across all of your cards is $10,000. In that case, your CUR is 20 percent. Lenders typically like to see low ratios of 30 percent or less.

Become an Authorized User on Another Account

Any account listed on your credit report could factor into your credit success. Let's say you have a friend or a family member with a great credit score. If they are willing, they could add you as an authorized user on a credit card, and each time they make a payment on time, it will positively affect your credit as well. Becoming an authorized *user* and *actually using* their credit are two different things. Let's keep it one hundred and honor the difference by sticking to just being authorized.

Real talk, the credit rebuilding process can be long and tiring, but once you see your FICO score improve, all of your efforts will be worth it. If you want a more detailed breakdown of the nuances of the credit repair process, I highly recommend the book *Perfect Credit: 7 Steps to A Great Credit Rating* by Lynnette Khalfani-Cox. If you don't have time to dispute the charges yourself, credit repair companies will take care of the heavy lifting for you. You will just want to carefully vet those companies and ask for references before agreeing to their services. Well, they won't do it on GP, but spending a little for significant credit improvement is worth it!

Now let's take that first step and pull your credit scores. You should ensure that this becomes an annual habit. Some experts even recommend pulling one report from each agency every four months.

Your Numbers
Credit Scores

. . . .

It's FREE to pull your credit scores once a year. Go to annualcreditreport.com and pull your full credit reports from the three credit score agencies—Experian, Equifax, and Transunion. Once you have your three credit reports, fill in the information below.

___

GOT SCORES?

Today's Date _____

___

EXPERIAN

Current Score _____ Goal Score _____

Is there any inaccurate information on your report?

Accounts in Adverse Standing (past due, bankruptcy, foreclosure, repossession, etc.) _____

Accounts in Good Standing _____

Utilization Rate _____ Years of Oldest Credit Line _____

___

EQUIFAX

Current Score _____ Goal Score _____

Is there any inaccurate information on your report?

Accounts in Adverse Standing (past due, bankruptcy, foreclosure, repossession, etc.) _____

Accounts in Good Standing _____

Utilization Rate _____ Years of Oldest Credit Line _____

TRANSUNION

Current Score [   ]   Goal Score [   ]

Is there any inaccurate information on your report?

Accounts in Adverse Standing (past due, bankruptcy, foreclosure, repossession, etc.) [   ]

Accounts in Good Standing [   ]

Utilization Rate [   ]   Years of Oldest Credit Line [   ]

Visit 7FigureNetWorth.com to print another copy of this form!

If, after pulling your scores, you recognize that you want to improve your scores, I again recommend you follow the detailed advice outlined in the book, Perfect Credit: *7 Steps to a Great Credit Rating* by Lynette Khalfani Cox.

Make a note in your calendar to pull your credit reports one year from now and notice the change.

Bragging Rights

Once you complete this step, we want to hear about it! Were you surprised by your credit scores? Did you see any information on there that you knew wasn't accurate? What steps, if any, are you planning to take to improve your scores? Share your answers in the #7-Figure Net Worth Facebook group.

CHAPTER NINE

Your Habits
6-Figure Shawn and 7-Figure Shonna

This is the story of two college classmates who landed entry-level jobs making $55K after graduation. Upon graduation, Shawn and Shonna each had approximately $18K in student loan debt. Bright and dedicated, each worked hard and eventually excelled at their jobs. Each received a 10% salary increase in the second year, bringing their salary from $55K to $60K.

In the third-year post-college, new opportunities began to shape for Shonna and Shawn. Both negotiated new salaries for managerial positions of $80K and $85K respectfully. During the fourth year, Shonna felt ready for greater leadership. She was happy to see herself on track to earn six figures before her 30th birthday due to anticipated annual performance increases. While Shawn's first company has been less generous, another company recognized his skills. In the fifth year, Shawn was tapped by another company to lead a new division with a hefty salary of $145K.

Before we move any further, let us take a closer look at Shonna and Shawn's personal financial decisions. We will start with Shonna.

As a preteen, Shonna's parents divorced. Her dad disappeared shortly after that, leaving her Mom to care for her and two younger brothers. Often her Mom struggled financially. Her mother would make ends meet by working multiple low-paying jobs. Since adulthood, Shonna felt obligated to send her Mom at least $300 per month to help support her brothers, who were now in high school. She continued to give the same amount even when her income grew. Shonna reasoned that while helping family was important, she also had to plan for the future. She promised herself she would never become anyone's financial burden.

Upon graduation from college, Shonna shared a three-bedroom apartment with two roommates in a less desirable yet safe part of town. The rent savings allowed her to make a larger monthly payment toward her student loans and accelerate full payoff. Shonna remembered her Grandpa always telling her, "Baby, owe no one anything but love." He deeply discouraged frivolous or heavy debts. She kept his words close to her heart. His words often came back to her when she saw free pizza and credit card offers during her years in undergrad. His words gave her the courage to say, "No, thanks," as she politely rejected credit card offers. Instead, she frequently headed to the student center where free financial classes were being offered.

It turns out the economics dean had a program where a professor would partner with a business leader each week to teach budgeting and money management to students. This volunteer rotation, officially called "The Art of Budgeting" provided Shonna and many other students with knowledge about managing their funds weekly.

As a working adult, Shonna reflected on the connection between Grandpa's wisdom and her budgeting classes. Even though she could afford an expensive high rise with her increased salary, she decided to upgrade to a moderately priced apartment with her roommates. This allowed her to have more funds to save for a down payment on a new home. As her down payment investment piled up, these funds represented peace of mind and a solid foundation to her.

Each month Shonna ensured that the automatic deductions flowed into a hard-to-reach bank account. She knew the temptation to overspend was real. So, she carefully concocted a way to prevent this from happening.

Through her times of reflection and prayer, she sensed that it was better not to have the debit card linked to her home down payment account just lying around in her apartment. In the past, that card had quickly left her secret stash and went into her wallet. She would then buy meals and clothes instead of eating leftovers and monitoring her savings.

Rather than keeping it around, Shonna decided it would be wise to lock it away in a safe deposit box nearly 50 miles away. It was only accessible after a one-hour drive to her Grandpa's hometown. She did not mind the hike since Grandpa was even more frugal than her, and it gave her a reason to visit and hear his stories. Whether Shonna realized it or not, he was one of her unofficial accountability partners.

Once she had saved enough to make a down payment, Shonna participated in a first-time homebuyer's program. She met with the program director and took another class to strengthen her budgeting and household management skills. The latter was necessary as Shonna saw the strengths and weaknesses of how her mother ran their childhood home. When she visited home, she gently introduced these concepts over meals with her Mom and brothers.

After reaching her down payment savings goal, Shonna purchased a duplex in need of "a little love" at $300K. After closing, her friends were so impressed by her financial strides that they asked to rent rooms in her home while preparing for their own homeownership. After weighing the benefits of living independently immediately versus increased income from renters, Shonna had a lawyer create two leasing agreements with her roommates. One roommate stayed a year until she purchased her own home—cross country. The other decided to stay two years until she improved her credit score before saving for her new home an hour away.

As a homeowner, Shonna's discipline for savings continued to grow. She loved watching cooking shows. She would practice meal prep on Sunday afternoons and carry lunches to work—Monday through Thursday. Friday, however, was the exception. On Fridays, she used her lunch hour to eat at a local restaurant with her work colleagues. Often, Shonna would observe conversations, and when asked, drop nuggets of wisdom about her financial journey. She did not want to cause a stir at work—yet many could not help but notice her difference.

Twice a year, Shonna set aside $1,800 for vacations. She often found great sales as she remained scrupulous in her travel deals. Driving the same used car she bought post-undergrad, this fully paid for vehicle was clean and maintained regularly. She found that the extra funds she could have spent on a new car note could go towards investments instead.

Shonna didn't remember when she was first introduced to compound interest. Yet she started investing early in her career. By reading a financial book each month, she gained enough financial understanding to know it was important to be intentional in this area. Writing bullet points of sound advice, Shonna made a habit of journaling every time she read something interesting. She increased her 401(k) contributions every year—until she maxed out her employer's matching percentage. While she occasionally splurged on shoes and gorgeous handbags; she learned quickly that these items were 'treats.' So, in her monthly budget, she designed a 'treat day' and every third Saturday she would go with her friends to shop. She often kept her purchases under a certain pre-budgeted amount.

After a recent promotion, Shonna decided to contact her financial advisor at her job. The HR representative mentioned that each employee could receive a 45-minute free session courtesy of the organization. Although her financial advisor did not go over her budget, he did generate a report based upon her current financial conditions. Using software programs with a Monte Carlo simulation, the advisor shared with her the potential gains of her investment portfolio. Reviewing the scenarios, he shared that If she continued her current performance path, Shonna would amass a net worth of over one million dollars in the following years, including the equity that was continually growing in her home.

Now, let's discuss Shonna's classmate from the same large university, Shawn. Shawn was raised by his Mom and Dad, who are still married. His uncle passed away after a prolonged illness when he was young, yet Shawn remained close to his aunt and cousins. His aunt has two sons and a daughter, all within five years of Shawn's age. Due to their proximity in age, Shawn's cousins were like brothers and sister to him—as he was the only child of his parents.

Within a couple of days after receiving his first job offer, Shawn headed to the car dealership. He loved cars, so he picked out a fully loaded four-door sedan that cost him about $31,000. He reveled in the 'new car smell' as he drove off the lot. Once a month, he headed to a car wash for a detail. The cost of this service was $170 a month. Once he settled into his new job, Shawn and one of his buddies rented an apartment in a modern high rise. He recalled how someone advised him to go cheaper. Yet Shawn figured that since he had a great job, he could enjoy the parties and nearby nightlife that suited him.

With his rent and car note taking up space in his wallet, Shawn opted to make the lowest monthly payment allowed on his student loans. For a while, living with his friends was fun but then it started to get a bit old. So upon his first promotion, Shawn moved out on his own to a trendy high rise in the center of the city's live-liest part. This raised his rent thirty–five percent (35%). To maintain his lifestyle, Shawn often just pulled out a credit card. He loved to entertain and ordered tons of food most Fridays when his friends or cousins came over. People assumed that Shawn was a baller, as he only cooked when he had the time and typically paid for everything when friends and family were out with him. Because Shawn was particular about his food, he would frequently head straight to his favorite restau-rant after work most weekdays.

When Shawn's cousins would fall short on their rents, they would often ask him to help out—promising yet again, "Cuz, you know I'm good for it. I'll pay you back as soon as I get my next check." The requests would often grow to include regular monthly expenses such as utilities, gas, or phone bills. Instead of setting a fixed amount, Shawn figured, *I can spare it.*

Before he knew it, he was quickly loaning $100 here and $300 there. After all, he thought, *We're family, right?* Yet Shawn did not account for word spreading quickly about his' generosity.'

Soon he was bombarded with calls, texts, and voicemail requests from other family members asking him to help out whenever they had a shortfall. Because he checked his account sporadically, Shawn reasoned that a few requests every now and then wouldn't break him.

Instead, Shawn decided to create a separate account where he deposited just enough to cover his bills—rent, utilities, car, minimum credit card, and student loan payments every month. He figured after that he could just spend the rest. He felt good about his financial situation and did not think about his spending beyond that because he knew he 'had' it.

He knew at his income level, he should probably be investing. So he purchased a few stocks using the apps suggested by a colleague. Every month he would pick a stock he personally liked and buy shares—as long as they did not exceed $200. Besides stock purchases, Shawn did not mind engaging in small talk about finances with friends as long as the discussion didn't get 'too deep.' Financial topics came up often—especially with work colleagues. Though he rarely acted on the sound ideas shared because he was embarrassed to admit that some information went over his head. On occasion, he would purchase a financial book and promise to read it. Yet before Shawn had time to dive in, something more interesting always seemed to come up.

He worked hard, and his new job allowed him to celebrate more often. He even earned a few bonuses that he immediately spent on 'luxury' splurges. After reaching the upper echelons of leadership in the company, Shawn decided it was time to upgrade his ride – so he did. A few months later, Shawn was hanging out with friends and offered to pay for the first round of drinks for seven of his buddies. He was shocked and embarrassed that, for some reason, his credit card was declined. Slightly shaken by the ordeal, Shawn quickly checked his account and realized he forgot about two purchases for new gadgets he covered for one of his cousins.

Noticing the discomfort and confusion on his face, his boy Julian graciously said, "Man, don't worry about it. I got it this time." He watched in amazement as his bro handled the bill. Later at a local coffee shop, he met up with Julian again. After a few minutes of catching up about mutual friends, Julian's face turned serious, and he asked Shawn if he had ever worked with a financial coach or planner. Shawn sheepishly shrugged his shoulders and mumbled no. He knew he needed help. His pride was strong, but good sense was slowly winning out. Julian, with an understanding expression, responded, "Man, I get it. This is the stuff no one talks about. My wife and I's finances were garbage last year until I sucked it up—and let somebody who knew what they were doing take a look at them." Shawn thought to himself, *I hate this! But I got to man up and handle my business before I go broke.* He agreed, and Julian arranged an introduction with their financial coach.

Usually, Shawn felt uncomfortable discussing finances this deeply with someone more knowledgeable than himself. Yet he had to be honest that he felt some relief when he saw the financial coach's meeting invitation come through on his calendar. After sitting down with the financial coach, Shawn realized that he was living a high-profile lifestyle with a negative net worth. Given the student loan payments and the credit card debt, Shawn realized that he had contributed very little towards his future so far. Worst yet, his gifts to family and friends were bleeding him dry. His retirement plans were minimal—and he had a mere $500 in savings. With the investment app that he had been using, he only gained $5K in 2 years.

Shawn was shocked! He thought his finances got him further than that!

Shawn decided enough was enough. He realized he had lost some time but was not without hope. His financial coach helped him create a monthly budget, and Shawn paid extra to direct all financial requests from family and friends through his new coach. The fee was no joke! But the freedom was indescribable. At first, Shawn's cousins and friends balked at these 'unloving' boundaries. They couldn't really fathom the loss that their requests and his compliance had inflicted on him.

Realizing ignorance was expensive, Shawn followed his coach's advice. He met up with some of his fellow alum at a local bookstore. There was a roster of teachers for budgeting classes and he noticed his old classmate "Shonna" was one of the instructors. After work, Shawn attended the weekly class to improve his financial IQ and emotional relationship with money. Every time he thought he had heard it all, he would be blown away by a new story of how someone overcame mistakes and financial ruin. Shawn realized he had to strengthen his fiscal management skills if he planned to get ahead.

The finale came when Shonna ended the 8-week budgeting session by sharing her personal story with the class. Shawn realized that this amazing woman, while different than himself, was someone he *had* to know better. 'Nuff said.

CHAPTER TEN

Your Habits
Monthly Budgeting & Reconciliation

> *"Fortunately, it's possible to . . . become a millionaire starting from nothing . . . I didn't win the lottery; I didn't inherit an estate. Rather, I was able to hit that milestone by identifying small life changes that can make a big financial impact."*
>
> *– Blake Konrardy, Author, Millennial Millionaire*

Let's get into some financial habits that can be very important to establish along your financial journey towards attaining a #7-Figure Net Worth—starting with budgeting and reconciling. I am not sure who speaks to you more—Shonna, who's crushing it, or Shawn, who's building his financial muscles, or perhaps like me, you see yourself as a blend of both. Regardless of where you may be starting, if they can do it, so can you! But you must decide, "I am going to build the habits that I need to win with finances—no matter what!"

So now that we have gotten intimate looks into the habits of Shawn and Shonna let's turn back the attention to the decisions and habits impacting your credits and debits—yes, your own. Listen! If we really undertake this march to achieve a #7-Figure Net Worth, we must cultivate both a healthy relationship *and* disciplined habits with money.

One of the first steps in really getting our money relationship right is consistently setting up a monthly budget. I get it . . . some of us may groan when we hear the b-word. Yet stick with me. Many of you may already have a monthly budget and a cadence for tracking your spending. If so, I applaud you. Keep up that great work. For those who have yet to realize its power, budgeting makes creating wealth creation a realistic process. It helps you see how your spending directly affects the progress towards your goals.

A reconciled monthly budget is a 28- to 31-day personal financial review where you can assess your financial habits during and after the budget is created. While evaluating the numbers, you can affirm positive financial habits and change any negative behavior that is leading to budgeting busting. Hmmm . . . I wonder what your common budget busters are. Before we go there, let us first deal with the emotional side of budgeting.

I Get Money!

When we think of budgeting, most of us may immediately feel restricted. I know I did! At times, my exact words were, "I worked hard for this money, and I should be able to spend it however I want to." Yeah, okay. I hear you and you *are* right to a certain extent. However, a budget helps you determine *how much*, *on what,* and *when* you should spend. It also shows you the opportunity cost of expending funds in one category versus another.

Listen! I know you *have* worked very hard for your funds. So *I am not* saying you should never go out and *spend money on depreciating assets like* Michael Kors bags, Movado watches, tools for your hobbies, red bottoms, or Italian cut designer suits, or whatever your splurge items look like. *I am* saying that these and all other purchases should be carefully planned, timed, and thought through.

Without a budget in place, right after a shopping spree, there could be a couple automatic drafts that you overlooked, resulting in your account being slammed with multiple $30–$40 overdraft fees. Suddenly, the shiny appeal of your purchases does not give off nearly as much light when you add that overdraft fee to its cost.

Yes, it is great to get a push notification to your phone whenever you swipe your card. Yet if you do not keep an accurate account of what is coming into your pocket and going out, you will quickly be upside down. This is a major financial issue! For example, in 2017, consumers paid more than $34 billion in overdraft fees. Stop and think about the *billions* being handled over to banks in part because we refuse to budget. I can only imagine what percentage black America has paid into those billions.

That is a lot of free money given away to banks! Especially when there are so many ways we could avoid these excessive charges. Aye, definitely no judging here—because I have paid my fair share. Yet, it has led me to have a greater recognition of the value of budgeting and disciplined spending. Budgeting is a powerful tool in our financial arsenal. At times it will definitely feel like a chore to some of us, yet over time you may find joy in tracking your finances consistently for your future. If nothing more—budgeting provides a fiscal blueprint for the realization of your dreams.

Tell Your Money What To Do!

Now, depending on your current financial situation, at first your budgeting and reconciliation may simply enable you to become cash flow positive every month or get a clearer picture of why you are constantly going into the red. You may not be in a situation where discretionary spending is the struggle. Instead, you are working on getting a handle on the timely payment of your basic obligations and achieving a positive monthly cash flow. That is a very important application of these habits as well!

Through budgeting, you will actually preserve more of your money by intentionally directing it at the outset into opportunities that can lead to financial freedom. When you create a budget each month, you give your money with an intention and direction to go forth and resolve your financial obligations and develop opportunities for abundance. This, in turn, allows you to pay your financial obligations on time, without losing opportunities, as you save and invest for the future without fear. Your money now has a focus! Your funds become aligned with your goals and dreams—and you earmark funds for investment vehicles that will cause your money to work directly for you!

Think of it this way—budgeting is a way of counting any cost before you engage in anything. For example, my faith has taught me the following:

> *For which of you, desiring to build a tower,*
> *does not first sit down and count the cost,*
> *whether he has enough to complete it?*
> *Otherwise, when he has laid a foundation*
> *and is not able to finish,*
> *all who see it begin to mock him, saying,*
> *'This man began to build*
> *and was not able to finish.'*
>
> *– Luke 14:28:30 (English Standard Version)*

What proverbial "tower" do you want to build in your life? What are you working toward building right now? What goals do you want to achieve? What are you saving for now? How will you feel once you are debt-free? What legacy do you want to leave your future generations, like your grandkids, nieces, nephews, cousins, or friends who feel like family touch your life?

Think about it. Seriously. What do *you* want to build? See, when we identify the amazing outcomes that we *can* achieve through budgeting—it has the potential to unlock the discipline growing inside of us. Once you realize that with each swipe you opt-out of because it is outside your allocated budget, you are not saying "No" to something. You are, in fact, saying a big "Yes!" to your larger financial goals. As you carefully assess each transaction you make, you are building your dreams one step at a time!

Reconciling Your Accounts

To shift our cultural mindset, budgeting is a concept that we must begin to teach early. I want us to teach our melanin babies to say, "I have x amount to spend because I used y amount to pay bills. I also put z amount away in savings and investment accounts." That is my hope and dream for this next generation. We have to teach the babies!

However, before we can effectively do so, we must make these concepts a component of our own adult realities first! That may not always be an easy task—even though it is abundantly worth it. With the advent of technology and online shopping, budgeting has become even more difficult. Hello, monthly Amazon "notes" (insert a dramatic eye roll)! It is easy to swipe your card or type in your card number and not think much about your funds because you "know" you have money in your account.

Even once you identify a specific budget amount for a particular category, you have to pair that with the discipline needed to spend only up to that allocated amount. For many of us, the real challenge comes in reallocating the way we spend our disposable income. If you are wondering what disposable income is (also called discretionary income), Intuit Turbo Tax explains how this is defined by any money you have after paying for your necessary expenses each month, like rent, transportation, food, utilities such as electricity, gas, or even healthcare-related expenditures.

As you transition from a freer approach of spending your disposable income to a strategic reallocation of funds into savings and investments, you may find the habit adjustments challenging. Despite the challenge and discomfort, many of us are indeed finding clever ways to stop the mindless spending.

For example, Prism's CEO, Tyler Griffin, insists there is a big change from how things were done 30 years ago. Griffin writes, "Back then you would take a few hours out in the evening, write checks for the mortgage, electric bill, phone bill, cable bill, and car loans, place them in envelopes and then balance the checkbook. You knew how much money was in your account when the next paycheck would come in and how much money was leftover." In short, taking time to write everything down or type it into a spreadsheet or app slows down the process allowing you to make better assessments of your finances.

Checking the Receipts

A few questions here. Have you ever taken a test in school and didn't receive a grade for it? Pointless, right? Why study? Why work extra hard on assignments? Why devote all your time to these activities without being able to see the fruits of your efforts? Budgeting can feel like that if you do not check your receipts—that is to reconcile your budget. If you refuse to hold yourself accountable by reconciling your spending each month, you are really undermining your budgeting efforts.

So, what *exactly* is reconciling? According to the Corporate Finance Institute, reconciliation is an accounting process used to prove that transactions—which add up to the ending balance—are correct. Moreover, when you reconcile, you bring your budget into a state free of inconsistency, difference, or conflict with your expenditures.

Reconciliation confirms that the sum leaving an account corresponds to the amount that is being spent. In this sense, it can be said that reconciliation is where two accounts are balanced and compared at the end of the reporting period—for budgeting, that would be every month.

In personal finance, it simply means comparing what you budgeted to what you actually spent! For example, in December, you may decide to spend $250 on holiday gifts and add that amount to your budget for the category of gifts. In January, for reconciliation purposes, you should review all of your transactions in December to see if that really happened! In our world, I would call it a new way to think about "checking the receipts." It is where your receipts match your budget!

So why is reconciling so important? Again, it is not always easy to be disciplined in spending. I get it 100%. On Friday, we see the direct deposit hit our accounts with a nice bonus. After that, it's time to enjoy the fruits of our labor. We go out and have a great meal with our friends, make a few impulse buys and call it 'enjoying life.' Why? Because we've earned it, and we deserve it. When Sunday evening rolls around and we check our accounts, we may be shocked to see that our direct deposit from Friday is now half gone. After staring blankly at the updated balance for a few moments, it may finally dawn on us that we failed the test of discipline. Now, we must wait two more weeks for another paycheck.

How do we prevent being seduced by the life of quick spending? How do we possibly stop those things? You guessed it—budgeting *and* reconciliation. ***We must build the habit of setting a budget for every dollar we receive, and we stick to it!***

When it comes to balancing your budget and reconciling, you can use your checking account statements and spreadsheets, finance apps, or online platforms like Mint. There are even people who budget with Google sheets. Regardless of the tool you use, you must establish a habit of building a budget each month *and* reconciling your spending against that budget at the end of each month.

You may take an old school practice (further back than AOL instant messenger) and follow the ledger practices our parents for reconciling their checks. The paper ledger documented what was spent and how much was left. In simple terms, a ledger allowed you to tally everything that went out and everything that went into your account. Another advantage is that you could easily see a missing bill or an unexpected expense with a ledger. Even in the digital world, sometimes, the manual process is still the best way. Whatever method you choose, the point is to pick the one you will consistently practice and just do it.

Grade the Test

Now, to help you get started, I have created a couple of worksheets that may help. The first is the **Monthly Budgeting Template**. There is also an excel version that you can download on our website 7FigureNetWorth.com. The second is a **Reconciliation Grade Sheet**. Let me keep it one hundred. I *may* have created this reconciliation grader just for me as I have been on the *monthly-reconcili-ation-struggle-bus* for a few months now! Besides, we can do this together by taking it one step at a time. If you track your monthly budget reconciliation, then you can assign a score and note your progress.

For example, if you are within your budgetary goals by 90–100 percent, you receive an "A" for that month. If, however, you are between 80–89 percent, you receive a "B" and so on. I know you remember that scale! The objective is to treat budgeting like a personal test where you hold yourself accountable for saving, investing, and spending. If you are ready, call up a friend and ask if they want to be your financial accountability partner. Then share your goal, and if comfortable, send them your budget reconciliation grades each month.

I know that some of you find personal finances . . . well, extremely personal. When challenges arise, you may feel ashamed and may be tempted to conceal your grades rather than share them. I want to encourage you to push through that discomfort.

I want you to succeed financially—so I am humbly asking you to work through each emotional, spiritual, and psychological challenge you face along this jour-ney. Don't just skip something because it's not in your current comfort zone. Identify a financial accountability partner that you can trust. Once you embrace fresh ideas and work through your struggles, you will be able to look back and see how far you have come. Trust me, you will do so with a smile when you come out on the other side.

The goal will be to reconcile your budget within days of the month's end. For example, you will want to reconcile your spending with January's budget by the 3rd day of February. You want to build this habit month after month to receive as many A's as possible.

While it may take a while to build a new habit of budgeting and reconciliation. Yet over time, you will find it worthwhile when you can have your month and money match (which I understand in some situations may take more than just budgeting). The effort will feel worth it as you begin to see those extra designated funds growing in your savings and investment accounts. You may also be surprised to find that you do not miss all that extra spending at all!

Having increasing income without financial success habits is not enough to generate enduring wealth. Many of us have been surprised to hear of wealth flowing through the hands of individuals who lost it due to poor decision-making. For example, ESPN Films released *Broke* on its 30 for 30 series. This show followed the heartbreak of quite a few NBA, NFL, and MLB players who lost millions, often in a relatively short amount of time.

We need to work to eliminate those types of heartbreaking stories within our community. So, let's start by keeping better track of our funds. It sure beats blindly swiping our cards and hoping for the best. You can build the habit of monthly budgeting and reconciling —because your financial future and your melanin minis are counting on you! A little discipline now can lead to a lot more play later. So let's get your numbers dropped into this monthly budget worksheet!

Your Habits
Monthly Budget

. . . .

MONTH		THIS MONTH'S BUDGETING GOALS

MONTH

EXPECTED MONTHLY INCOME

STARTING CHECKING BALANCE

THIS MONTH'S BUDGETING GOALS

1)

2)

3)

EXPENSES

CATEGORY	DESCRIPTION	AMOUNT	BUDGETED	EXPENDED

MONTH OVERVIEW

TOTAL INCOME	
TOTAL EXPENSES	
MONTHLY CASH FLOW	

DOWNLOAD THE EXCEL
FOR THIS WORKSHEET AT
7FIGURENETWORTH.COM

PASSWORD: 7FNW

Your Habits
Reconciliation Grade Sheet
....

Let's take it back to a grading scale like we had in middle school. Back when, you would grab capri suns, flamin' hot cheetos, and lemonheads from the neighborhood "candy lady." It worked then and it will work for us now!

A	90–100%
B	80–89%
C	70–79%
D	60–69%
F	50–59%

MONTH	DATE RECONCILIATION COMPLETED	BUDGET AMOUNT	SPENT AMOUNT	% W / IN BUDGET	GRADE THIS MONTH

CHAPTER ELEVEN

Your Habits
Debt Reduction

> *"Just because you can afford the payments doesn't mean you can afford the item."*
>
> *– Unknown (wise person, though!)*

One of the key aspects of building positive and then high net worth is eliminating and then not rebuilding your debt. However, this particular principle of debt reduction is often less about knowledge and education and more about your everyday habits and choices.

On your road to financial freedom, you must understand how to be released from the burden of debt. If you want to take actionable steps to lighten or eliminate your debt, there are more than a few ways to get it done. I created an acronym to help you remember the debt reduction strategies that I suggest.

W	**- Why do you want to be debt-free?**
E	**- Exercise new habits that align with your financial goals.**
A	**- Accumulate a savings cushion for opportunities and unexpected events.**
L	**- Leverage additional income streams to pay down debt faster.**
T	**- Take one debt at a time.**
H	**- Have those tough conversations.**

W – Why do you want to be debt-free?

What motivates one person to take action and make a change can be completely different from person to person. Regardless of the variance, there is tremendous power in starting your journey to become debt-free with a clear understanding of your reason why. In his book about business leadership, *Start with Why*, Simon Sinek shares, "When they are unclear about your WHY, WHAT you do has no context." This can be true in personal finance, as well. So take a moment to identify all of the reasons why you want to be debt-free.

How will you feel? Will it relieve stress, bring joy, or give a feeling of freedom? What will you be able to accomplish? Where will you be able to go? Who will you be able to give to or impact? Understanding the outcomes you are working towards will help you keep pushing on those days where you may feel like slacking off. For me, I knew that I wanted to be debt-free because I wanted to start saving for my kid's future. Why do *you* want to pay off *your* debt?

E – Exercise new habits that align with your financial goals.

You must take a close look at each of your debts. Perhaps, pulling out the credit reports you identified earlier may be a great place to start. Take a look at each debt and think about the circumstances that led to that debt. Was it an unexpected situation? Was it a lack of resources? Was it a desire that you chose to indulge? Was it a pattern of spending that repeated? Not all incurred debt is rooted in poor habits or decisions but it is important to identify those that are. When you look back at your debt, are there any habits you can identify contributing to your current debt situation? What new habits can you replace them with?

When I started my debt-free journey, it consisted primarily of a used car loan, student loans, and credit card debt. My car was purchased with relatively low mileage with a great used car warranty and was two model years old. It was a car that was known for reliability and to last a long time. Looking back, I felt confident about that choice, and the only change I would make today would be to save up and then instead buy a car with cash.

My student loan debt was mostly for graduate school. I would growl at that debt. Looking back, I wish I had researched more about scholarships and other schools that offered similar degrees with a one-year program instead of two years. The new habits that I started after this reflection were carefully research-ing, comparing, and vetting all significant financial decisions. The approach I will share in an upcoming chapter about examining your mortgage product as much as or equal to the effort you put into finding a physical home is an exam-ple of that.

Finally, my credit card debts. Boy! That was where the behavioral land mines were. Looking back, I knew that I had swiped my card far too many times for meals with friends, for an outfit to a new event, or for travel. Instead of owning up or being transparent about my financial situation, I opted to use resources that I didn't have to "keep up." The new habit that I employed was honesty and self-denial. I started being honest with family and friends about where I was in my financial journey. I either declined offers to go to dinner or ate beforehand and would just order a side dish or an appetizer during the meal. I found honesty to come much easier than self-denial.

Whew! Delayed gratification and self-denial can be huge new habits to help you execute a successful debt reduction strategy. Those were the most important and the hardest for me. Instead of buying a new outfit, I learned to borrow or mix and match existing pieces. Instead of joining on a trip that I couldn't afford, I opted out. Instead, I created a bucket list for when I was in a better financial situation. It may mean that you first identify all the areas where you may need to exercise re-straint. If that means you don't buy that new gaming system right when it comes out, wearing those stilettos for two seasons, letting go of those season tickets, or even taking a hard look at those luxury grocery items. You may opt to find more affordable farmer's markets instead of defaulting to your primarily organic grocery stores for a season. Whatever it may be for you, it will likely take sacrifice—and that is a fair exchange for becoming debt-free. When you take an honest look at your current debt situation, what new habits can you exercise to reduce and en-sure you don't re-incur debt?

Stop Creating More Debt

Okay, this should go without saying, but I will say it anyway because somebody needs to hear it—you don't need a new credit card. I know it is tempting when you get that low APR deal sent straight to your mailbox. The temporary card is shining underneath the light and on the envelope, it reads, "You Are Approved" in big, bright red letters. Please, let those red letters caution you to STOP. Step away from the letter. If you want to get out of a hole, would you get a shovel and dig your way out? Or would you figure out a way to climb to the top? Don't dig yourself deeper. Think for a way up—and out. Throw that letter in the shredder right away!

A – Accumulate a savings cushion for opportunities and unexpected events.

A car breaks down, a refrigerator goes out, a last-minute plane ticket is needed. Sometimes life just happens. However, the best defense against needing to incur debt in these situations is to build a savings cushion of $500 or $1,000. That way, you can rely on your cash instead of needing to swipe your card when an unexpected opportunity or event comes your way. We will talk a little more about this in the *Intentional Savings* chapter.

L – Leverage additional income streams to keep a positive cash flow and pay down debt faster.

Debt can sometimes not just be rooted in habits, but more so in inadequate resources. If you find yourself using credit cards to bridge the gap between your income and expenses, then you likely have a cash flow problem. If you have already examined your habits and got your budget down to bare bones, next you will want to explore ways to increase your active income stream (such as asking for a raise—if deserved—from your employer). Also, identify additional income sources that you can add to your household budget to achieve positive cash flow. We will discuss options for this in the *Multiple Income* chapter.

T – Take one debt at a time.

When you look at your credit report, you may get overwhelmed by the debts you see. I know you may be looking at certain line items like—how in the world did I neglect to return a $40 piece of cable equipment that I now owe $530 for? Yes, that is how debt creeps upon us. Something small quickly turns into an absurdity. However, this is when you should take things one debt at a time. Don't look at everything on your plate and try to eat it all at once. There are multiple approaches to paying off debt that allow you to take it one debt at a time. Three of the most popular ones are:

Snowball method – With this method, you line up your debts from the smallest to the largest. You pay them off in that order. With the first debt that you take, you pay the most you can above the minimum on that one debt while paying the minimum payment amount on all others. Once you have knocked out the smallest debt, you now use that old payment amount toward your next one on the list. This allows you to build momentum in your debt payoff process—so you have a larger "snowball" to throw at each debt consecutively.

Avalanche method – This approach is similar to the snowball method, except you line your debts up by the one with the highest interest rate to the lowest and pay off your debts in that order.

Tsunami method – With this strategy, you line up your debts based on the one with the highest emotional debt to the one that has the least emotional impact on you. With this method, you may opt to pay off your first couple of high emotional impact debts using this method. Then realign your debts after that based on the snowball or avalanche approach if your remaining debts have a similar level of emotional impact.

Regardless of which approach you take, just take it one debt at a time.

H – Have those difficult conversations.

Understand that if you want to transform your financial future, at some point, you are going to have to find and wear your "big girl panties" or "your big boy drawls." That means you may have to have some difficult conversations. We just talked about the difficult conversations you may need to have with yourself. Now let's talk about the tough discussions you may need to have with others.

Talk to your creditors – Listen, debt collectors can be intimidating people. You may have become a pro at recognizing their numbers, blocking, pretending to be someone else, or speak another language (no hables ingles.) No, that's not y'all? Just your cousins and 'nem? Whether you take a creative approach to dodging the calls or not, it is important to simply talk to your creditors—understanding that at times it may be difficult. Talk about your payment terms, tell them when you intend to pay and find out if there are any special programs or offers you may be able to take advantage of.

Dispute Charges – Debt has a statute of limitations, meaning there is only a certain amount of time that debts can stay on your report. It is typically 7 years. If you come across a debt that should have dropped off your credit by now, dispute the charge and have it removed. Research the statute of limitations for the debts on your credit report. You may discover that some debts are remaining there illegally. Use vigilance because you don't want to miss a chance to improve your credit and erase a debt at the same time.

Negotiate – Some people love a good negotiation and some, well . . . find it quite difficult. So, let's say you have debt on your report and it is legit. But the problem is that it is well above what you can pay in one lump sum. Again, there is a way you can handle it—and that is by answering the phone. There is a chance that your creditor may be willing to settle for much less than what you owe. So either *ahem* again, answer the phone or find the number on your statement or collection notice and give that creditor a call. Regardless of how uncomfortable it may feel, this is a difficult conversation worth having.

The road to becoming debt-free will have several components but it is definitely work you can and should do. My husband and I started our journey six-figures plus in the negative, so if we can do it, so can you. We used these methods, leveraged our community's support and worked with a financial coach, which we will discuss in a subsequent section.

Let's use this next worksheet to get our minds and habits right so we can get our money right too! With the right focus and sacrifice, you can also be living debt-free in no time.

Your Habits
Debt Reduction
· ·

1. Being honest with yourself, look at the quote beginning this chapter. What, if any, items/services are you paying for, but given your financial situation and goals, if you had to pay the entire balance today, could you not actually afford?

2. Why do you want to achieve a debt-free life? What new feelings would you have if you were able to make this a reality?

3. What old habits have kept you in debt? Which of these stagnant habits is going to be the hardest to break? Why?

4. What new habits will you introduce into your life to take the place of the stagnant habits that have been holding you back?

5. In preparing for the unpredictability of life, do you currently have a savings cush-ion to help with unexpected expenses? If so, how much? If you don't at least have a $500 cushion, if you were to make some small (or big) sacrifices starting today, by what date could you establish an initial cushion of at least $500?

6. Access your credit report and review the three most popular debt reduction methods (Snowball, Avalanche, Tsunami) discussed in this chapter. After exam-ining your credit report, which of the three methods give you the most motiva-tion to start reducing your debt? Why did you choose this method?

7. On your debt reduction journey, the most important and often most difficult con-versation you need to have is with yourself. Write yourself an honest and moti-vational email that speaks to admitting past mistakes, growing and getting rid of bad habits, and finally making moves to achieve financial goals. Write down how this new journey feels and how it is going to change your life. Please, don't beat yourself up for past decisions. Remind yourself that you are on a new journey, and you are finally on a better path—towards an intended destination. Send this email to yourself and save it as a favorite or leave it unread every time you read it. Whenever you need a reminder, it will always be there for you.

8. In addition to having a difficult conversation with yourself, you also need to have difficult conversations with others. Many people are professional in the way they avoid speaking to their creditors. It's understandable because this is often very uncomfortable for many reasons. What thoughts, feelings, and assumptions have kept you from talking to your creditors?

9. Speaking again about creditors, this conversation is easy to avoid. You can choose to never answer an unrecognized number, BUT that was the old you. To prepare to answer that next call (or even take the step in calling them yourself), write down a list of questions you want to ask your creditors. Start with the questions from this chapter (payment terms, special programs, etc.) to help keep you comfortable and confident during this conversation.

10. Referring to your credit report again. Are there any charges you may need to dispute? Research the statute of limitations, then take the necessary steps to dispute those charges.

CHAPTER TWELVE

Your Habits
Multiple Income Streams

> *. . . Invest in seven ventures, Yes, in eight;*
>
> *You do not know what disaster may come upon the land.*
>
> *– Words of King Solomon in Ecclesiastes 11:2 (New International Version)*

Many of us may be familiar with the character on the 1990's television show Martin by the name of Hustle Man. If you aren't, I think his name gives you insight into his character. I think he is most famous for trying to sell Martin a stick of rotisserie chicken while everyone was stuck inside their homes during a Detroit blizzard. Yes, the character was a part of a sitcom, but he had one thing in mind—multiple streams of income. He knew that doing one thing wasn't going to cut it. He had to put together numerous ventures if he wanted to make money.

You've Got to Hustle, Man

Nobody likes to lose income, but what's worse is losing income when there is nothing to supplement the loss. Having multiple streams of income is equivalent to having a spare tire in your ride. If you happen to catch a flat, all you have to do is put the spare tire in its place. Is it as durable as the original tire? Probably not, but it *will* get you to your destination. That is precisely what multiple streams of income are designed to do. They are your "spare tires" of finances.

I get it. Many of us work our 9–5 shifts and come home tired with no energy to do anything except lay on the couch and watch TV. Those with children and/ or spouses also have to have the opportunity to pour into them. After wearing all of our hats, we can be completely exhausted by the end of the day. We may feel like we don't have the energy to put into another income stream that requires any additional physical or intellectual effort. However, in today's landscape, we have to push past that feeling and hustle, man.

According to IRS tax filing information, the average millionaire in the United States has seven income streams. Regarding this concept, if you had to name seven (7) income-generating ventures to include in your personal financial portfolio right now, what will your streams be? Look closely at your opportunities. Coupled with your skills and abilities, what could you do to create additional income streams?

Whether it is a "side hustle," creating an online course, or a real estate investment—you must find a way to identify other sources of income beyond your primary work. In our personal financial journey, we have learned to establish a mix of passive and active income streams. Passive income streams as earnings that come towards you in which you are not actively involved in generating. Think of limited business partnerships, rental properties, royalties from a book, and other ventures where you have minimal involvement. It is important to note that there may be some initial period that requires your active participation for many passive streams. In one of my friend groups, we call this "pillow money" because it's money you make even while sleeping. When it comes to multiple income streams, you should aim to add active *and* passive income streams. Let's talk about a few ideas that may get your creative money-making wheels turning when it comes to developing multiple streams of income in your life.

Ideas for Additional Income Streams

1. Entrepreneurship

> **"So our people not only have to be reeducated to the importance of supporting black business, but the black man himself has to be made aware of the importance of going into business. And once you and I go into business, we own and operate at least the businesses in our community.**

What we will be doing is developing a situation wherein we will actually be able to create employment for the people in the community. And once you can create some employment in the community where you live it will eliminate the necessity of you and me having to act ignorantly and disgracefully, boycotting and picketing some practice some place else trying to beg him for a job."

– Malcolm X

Let's first talk about building your own business as a source of income. Entrepreneurship in America is essential, but even more so, black entrepreneurship. Why? Because with our unemployment rates always being twice as high as our white counterparts, it signals that it may be time for more of us to go into business on our own. Sure, we may laugh at Hustle Man when we see him on Martin, but in the heart of his act is truth.

Take a moment to consider if the route of entrepreneurship is one you would want to pursue.

It doesn't have to start on a full-time basis. You can create a business on a part-time basis that could grow into a full-time opportunity over time. You could also opt to keep a job full-time and continue working a business part-time. Many people do this by turning a hobby or something they are very good at into a side hustle. Say it with me: *options*!

Start with a focus on your best talents that will maximize your energy for establishing additional income streams. What do people always say that you are good at or give you compliments on? What activities do you do that you quickly lose track of time with? Focusing on the intersection of your talent and your passion is critical here.

In his study of 60 millionaires that was the basis of his book *Millionaire Next Door*, Thomas J Stanly noted that "there is a direct positive correlation between the love of one's vocation and level of net worth." When we hear the stories of people achieving exceptional financial success levels, they often point to a passion project or hustle. They started it on the side and then poured into its exponential growth over time. One question to ask yourself now is, "What talent(s) do I possess that could be provided to others at a reasonable cost?" List at least one thing or as many talents as you like.

Listen, we don't have to just get involved in entrepreneurship solely to increase our personal financial gain (although that's okay too). We can also use our businesses to address pressing needs in society. Social entrepreneurship is when a company is started to meet a societal need or address a problem and not solely in for profit. I am continually learning that my own skills and experiences can be converted into income-generating businesses while also helping others. The book that you are reading right now is an apt example.

Direct Sales and Multilevel Marketing

A great way to get introduced to entrepreneurship while also being provided with hands-on training and support is through direct sales and multilevel marketing companies. This is an additional income source I have personally integrated into my own life. Regarding multilevel marketing (MLM), a Forbes article notes the legitimate ones compensate a person well who is willing to *work hard*. The article notes that while MLMs are at times erroneously referred to as "pyramid schemes," others have proven that nothing is farther from the truth. As a direct marketing millionaire, Stormy Wellington explained to Ebony magazine that she advocates direct sales' advantages given its compensation. If you do not want to put in the effort to start an entire business from scratch, this is a great way to start. It provides entrepreneurship with a roadmap and infrastructure already in place.

Support Is a Verb

While we are on the topic, let me dust off and hop on my soapbox for a quick moment. "Ahem." She said and cleared her throat. Speaking from my diaphragm and saying it loud to make my ancestor Malcolm X proud. When black businesses pop up, we <u>have to do better</u> at supporting them. Black businesses create *black money* that should have an opportunity to remain in *black hands*. Take a look at Tidal (a black music streaming service) and Apple. Tidal offers more royalties per plays than Apple, but they don't have nearly as much business. Why? The answer is beyond me, but <u>if we were always extremely intentional to support our own, we would be much better off than we are now</u>.

We have to do better when our people create businesses —myself included. Many other communities seem to get it, but far too often, we still struggle in this area. An easy example may be right in your bathroom. Are there any products that you regularly purchase from the drug store that you could buy from a small, well-run black-owned business instead? This is just one example of an extra step we could all take to be more intentional about giving one another support. *She steps down from her soapbox and carries on.*

2. Investing

Stock Market

The stock market is a great way to create additional income streams if you decide to focus on income-producing stocks. There are multiple ways to get involved with stocks, but this will take a little bit of time and research to understand how everything works. Various sources provide free information on things like day trading, stocks with dividends, and index funds to get you on the right track. Go to YouTube and type in "income-producing stocks" and similar search terms. The key answers you need to get started could be found in a few short videos. Now, wouldn't that be a worthwhile tradeoff for giving up time you would have spent watching a few of your favorite Netflix shows? I would venture to say yes.

3. Real Estate

Investing in real estate is a multi-faceted venture. With so many ways to get involved, you may get frustrated when you realize you don't know where to begin. Below, you will find a few different types of real estate investments you may want to put your money into.

Buy and Hold Real Estate

Buy and hold real estate is a strategy where you purchase a property with the intent to keep it in your investment portfolio for an extended period. You would typically rent it out until you decide to sell it. If you don't have the cash to pay the full purchase price upfront, this strategy may you require you to:

1. have funds to cover for a down payment and

2. the credit/income to qualify for a mortgage.

Most lenders will provide you with capital for up to ten financed properties. It blew my mind when I found that out!

You want to be thoughtful about how you leverage such an opportunity. However, with a detailed and well-researched plan—you could set out on your path to acquire one or multiple rental properties. You will start telling your friends, "Just call me landlord."

If you don't have the time to fully embrace all the work associated with being a landlord, it's alright. There are professional property managers that will manage your property for you for around 10 percent of the monthly rent.

Flipping a house

I think we can thank the HGTV (Home and Garden Television) channel for making the concept of flipping houses so mainstream. There are several shows that, in 30 minutes, make the process look so simple. Flipping a house typically means buying a house at below market value, investing money, and managing the process to renovate. Then selling it immediately and ideally for a profit. To the show producers' credit, some episodes show the agony of going over budget, selling to break even or at a loss, or not being able to sell at all. While there are pitfalls and risks to plan for, there are multiple examples of how this can be a viable way to generate additional income. I have several friends who have been able to increase their net worth with this strategy.

If this is a route that you want to go, definitely do your homework. If possible, for your first one or two projects, see if there is someone locally that you can partner with or serve as a mentor to show you the ins and outs of this strategy. From financing to building a reliable construction crew to finding a consistent flow of inventory, there will be multiple steps that you will have to cultivate and design. However, when carefully done—there can be a significant profit at the end of the process that can positively contribute to your net worth.

Wholesaling

You may have noticed signs on the side of the road or billboards that say, "We want to buy your ugly house." or "We will pay cash for your house." It's not because the buyers just want an ugly home—they actually want to wholesale it to a buyer interested in flipping it into something appealing. Then sell it so that they receive a profit on the investment.

The buyer usually pays a higher price than the seller accepted as the purchase price. The wholesaler keeps the difference as profit. It can be time-consuming. However, if you can identify the right property, buyers, and sellers, it is a great option to add additional income into your portfolio with far fewer upfront costs than other real estate strategies.

Creating a basement apartment

Do you have extra space in your basement (below your home and/or office building), and you don't know what to do with it? A basement apartment is just that—a space situated below the street level that is converted to a rental unit. There are special requirements and regulations for this type of rental. Once you comply with local rules, your basement apartment can create a steady monthly income stream.

Join a real estate investment group

If you don't have the capital available to make real estate purchases on your own, then this may be an ideal option for you. A real estate investment group is formed when people pool their money to purchase properties.

4. Write a Book or Create an Online Course

A great book can create a continual source of income. Numerous authors make a six-figure salary from book publishing alone. There are steps to it, though. You can't just write a book and expect it to suddenly generate thousands of dollars from revenue or royalties. A good marketing plan is needed to ensure that your content reaches the right people. However, if the plan is solid, all you need is a good niche to flow in. Take some time and think about things your industry needs. Perhaps you can offer advice or develop a self-help topic that would be beneficial to many. Your knowledge can become revenue in more ways than one.

If writing a book isn't your thing, then take a shot at creating online courses for your area of expertise, or you could do both. If you have developed a name for yourself and people seek you for different technical or non-technical "how-to" advice, create an online course and "sell" your knowledge.

At the end of the day, we all want to be in a better position financially. If we can learn anything from Hustle Man, the lesson would be it's not only about what you make; it's also about how many ways you can make it. With this next worksheet, let's identify some possibilities that may lead you to additional income streams.

Your Habits
Multiple Income Streams
· ·

1. If you were to lose your primary source of income today, do you have anything in place to help supplement that loss? If not, write down how that makes you feel and how that would impact yourself and your family.

2. How many income streams do you currently have?

3. In light of learning that the average millionaire in the US has seven income streams, how many would you like to have? Given your work and personal life, what is a realistic timeline to reach this goal?

4. One of the challenges of creating multiple income streams while still working a 9–5 is finding time and energy to set up the streams. But you may have more time than you think. For the next 7 days, do the following:
    a. Document all the tasks and activities (chores, watching TV, sleeping, spending time with family, talking on the phone, social media, etc.) you do in a single day and week, outside of your regular job.
    b. Write down the time you spend focusing on these things.

    c. Cross out the less critical tasks than developing your streams of income and could be considered a time-waster.

    d. Re-evaluate your list. Add up the time you now have available after eliminating those activities. Can you now identify time to set up your multiple streams of income?

5. Write down three hobbies or interests you have with more knowledge or experience than the average person?

6. If you are currently an employee, becoming an entrepreneur can be a great income source while doing something you love. If time and finances were not an issue, what business would you start today?

7. If time and finances are a challenge, how can you modify your goal and start your business on a tiered scale (i.e., start with one product or service and expand from there)? Take into account the amount of time and money you can invest or raise to get started.

8. The stock market is an excellent source of passive income, but it takes a little time on the front end to get started. While it can be confusing initially, you don't have to have a business or economics degree to understand how it can work for you. To get started on your journey into the stock market, do these three things:

a. Search for and subscribe to a podcast about the stock market and commit to listening to it weekly (**take notes**).

b. Find and subscribe to a YouTube channel with tons of content about the stock market you can learn daily (**take notes**).

c. Find a book or audiobook about investing in the stock market and carefully read or listen (**again . . . take notes**).

9. Think about your hobbies and interests you wrote down in question 4. How can you turn **each** of these into an additional income stream? Then, think about which one you can see yourself doing successfully, comfortably, and joyfully for the rest of your life. Which one feels the best?

10. Everyone has essential knowledge or a story to share with the world. Believe it or not, there is an audience for every topic imaginable.

a. What topic can you write a book about if you really put in the effort?

b. What would be a fun title for the project?

c. Now do this, open your word processor (Microsoft Word, Google Docs, Pages, etc.). On that blank page, go down to the middle of the page and center your text. Now, type in the title you created. Under that title, write By: (Enter Your Name).

11. Take a look. You have an idea and a title. You are already two steps closer to authoring and selling your book—a book that someone needs to read and could earn you income for the rest of your life.

12. Reread the Malcolm X quote. Focus on two things he says, "the black man him-self has to be made aware of the importance of going into business" and "actu-ally creating employment for the people in the community." Do you agree with Malcolm's thoughts here? Why or why not? If you do, how can you help make this a reality in your own community?

13. Have you ever considered real-estate investing as a real possibility for yourself? If you haven't made that step yet, conduct an online search for real estate classes in your local area. Also, search for online courses to help you get started (i.e., YouTube, Coursera, etc.). Next, complete a search for ways to get funding for real estate ventures. What useful information did you find? From the information you discovered, write down the first action you will take to begin investing in real estate as a semi-passive income stream.

The key here is:

Don't wait to take action when it comes to multiple income streams.

Learn a little, then take a little action.

Learn some more, take more action.

Grow from there!

CHAPTER THIRTEEN

Your Habits
Intentional Savings

> *"The art is not in making money, but in keeping it."*
>
> *– Proverb*

Being very transparent, writing this section is definitely tough because, in the past, I did *not* naturally save. This was an area where I honestly had to PUT IN WORK to transform. I had to proactively rewire my mind and confront stagnant money mindsets cultivated from the concepts I was exposed to during my upbringing. In my household as a kid, we were counting change just to buy meals, juggling which utility bill to pay each month, and fighting eviction notices. The idea of savings cushions and emergency funds was totally foreign to me. The reality of "just trying to make it" through that next week or month was stuck in my thinking.

Thank goodness for the financial education that opened my eyes. I learned from book mentors like Glinda Bridgforth's *Girl Get Your Money Straight*, Dave Ramsey's *Total Money Makeover,* and Crown Financial Ministries' materials. My husband, alongside my financial coach, have been great sources of support in helping me transition to a mindset of insightful financial decision-making. With the guidance, education, and support of these resources, I was able to renew my mind on the importance of establishing a:

1. baseline emergency fund of $1,000

2. short-term emergency fund with one (1) month of expenses, and

3. long-term emergency fund with three (3) to six (6) months of expenses with the exact number of months being determined by your risk tolerance, responsibilities, and steadiness of your line of work.

Without substantial savings today, I would feel completely exposed. Boy, is that growth! That's a massive mindset shift for me from my starting point of just trying to make it through each month and each week without being too hungry and the utilities still being on. Now, as an adult with my own family, our savings serves a defense against hard or uncertain times, and I feel more at ease.

Some of you may be completely different from me and savings come naturally. For example, my oldest daughter is a natural saver. She loves seeing her money stack up and won't spend any of it until she reaches a specific numerical goal. Even then, she will try to talk her father and me into spending *our* money on something she wants before she spends her own. You may identify with her—you may have multiple accounts—and love seeing those numbers rise further. You can live frugally in favor of seeing your funds grow.

Whether you are a natural saver like my oldest daughter or a natural spender like me, developing a habit of intentional savings is a critical component of your #7-Figure Net Worth strategy. Most financial advisors and coaches will recommend a baseline goal of saving at least 10% of your income. I recognize that in some situations, such a savings plan is easier said than done. If you are in the all too familiar position right now of having more month than money. In that case, there are initial steps you can take before you can begin your intentional savings path.

#BuildYourEmergencyStash

As I mentioned earlier, I highly recommend placing the words "Dave Ramsey emergency fund" in a search engine to read articles and watch media related to this idea. There is no point in me reinventing the wheel here. He has done a great job on this topic. Dave shares creative ways of building your first $1,000 emergency fund, from starting a second job to selling depreciating assets that drain your monthly cash flow—such as financed cars.

If you have to get creative to get that first stash built, remember your journey of a thousand miles starts with taking the first step. No matter how far you are from the goal line, you can start with $10 a month if that is where you are. If you happen to be in a better position to save more— go ahead and start with that commonly espoused baseline of saving at least 10% of your income. Then, work with a financial coach to see where you want to go from there.

In positions of surplus, barely enough, or depletion, it will be important to take a hard look at your monthly budget after reconciling. Identify any areas where you can reduce spending. That may mean participating in local and free activities to spend less on your entertainment. You may start couponing to save on groceries, or you may cut your cable bill and use a cheaper streaming service. During a lean season, our family had a blast couponing, and to this day, my daughter will exclaim if she sees me throw a coupon in the trash. This phrase does not wear out—*where there is a will, there's a way*!

If you are determined to build the habit of saving, you will find funds or add income sources to position yourself to do so. Call your internet and cell phone provider to find out if there are any promotions. Cut down on costs associated with eating out by packing your lunch or eating beforehand at home and just ordering an appetizer when going out with friends. Believe me! We have done *all of this* and more on our financial journey to become debt-free and increase our net worth! There are so many ways to live an abundant life while also preserving your resources. Your aim will be to find creative ways to pay off any existing debt and build your emergency funds.

#BLACK*Millennial* ADULTING

Identify three or four budget categories that you can trim to increase your budget's savings and/or investment portions. Even if you already have a positive cash flow each month with money earmarked for savings and investing. You can still identify additional funds that can be *better* used to accelerate your #7-Figure Net Worth journey.

Find us on Facebook

 What budget categories have you decided to trim? Share one or two items that you have decided to trim on our #7-Figure Net Worth Facebook group and your accountability partner. If you feel comfortable, feel free to share the prior amount and the current amount. Or, if you choose to be discreet, share the before and after percentage change. Again, keep in mind that you may never know who may see your post, learn from you, and be inspired to make a change themselves.

Technology + Savings

There are also multiple ways to leverage technology for sufficient savings. Consider the following tech-driven approaches to savings:

• Automatic Deductions @ the Bank – Set exact amounts. You could also enroll in a program that rounds each purchase up to the dollar and automatically places the difference in a savings account.

• Savings apps like Acorn, Stash, Clink, Betterment, etc.

• Online money market accounts to gain an additional point or two of interest on your emergency funds.

What is your favorite tech-enabled savings app?

 Share with us on Instagram. Take a screenshot and tag @WisdomThenWealth. Don't forget to use the hashtags #7FigureNetWorth and #BuildYourEmergencyStash

Your Habits

Intentional Savings

1. Review your past 3 monthly financial statements. What percentage of your monthly income do you allocate for savings right now?

2. If you can comfortably increase this amount, what percentage of your monthly budget will you begin to allocate to savings starting next month?

3. What is the percentage of your monthly budget that you desire to allocate every month (goal percentage)? List three action steps you will take to help you get to that goal percentage and identify the date you will complete or implement this change.

4. What is the current interest rate on your savings account? If you are unsure, contact your bank, and while you have them on the phone or online chat, make sure you are receiving the highest rate possible. Never hurts to ask, right?

5. It's a smart money move to have enough funds in your savings to cover at least 3 months or more of monthly expenses. Once in place, you will likely want to place your funds in a money market account to gain the highest growth benefit from those funds. Research your local banks, credit unions, or other financial institutions and decide which money market account you will place those funds in. What will your interest rate be on that account?

6. What additional savings goals do you have? Identify 5–6 savings goals that you would like to reach.

7. With a mindset of "what gets scheduled is what gets done," add the desired time frame for each goal. Be sure to include at least two "stretch" goals that go above and beyond your current expectations of achievements. For your first goals, it may be "I want to have my 1–month rainy day fund in place within the next 6 months" or "I want to save $50,0000 for a first (or second/vacation) home down payment within the next two years." For your stretch goal, it may be something like, "I want to save $22,000 cash to purchase a used vehicle with cash." Or "I want to have a mix of savings and investments of $600,000k available to liquidate and purchase a single–family home in cash within the next two years."

8. Now that you have had the time to think about it, it's time to follow the lead of Habakkuk 2:2, to write the vision, make it plain, then make it happen. What are your savings goals?

1.

2.

3.

4.

5.

6.

CHAPTER FOURTEEN

Your Habits
Impactful Giving

> *"Don't wait until 'someday later' to serve the world. Don't wait until you're richer than Oprah or Bill Gates. Don't wait until you have more connections or more of whatever you think you need. Begin now. No matter your age or economic status, you have something that you can share. Become a mentor and teach what you have learned . . . Become a philanthropist or champion a cause."*
>
> *– Karen Arrington, Author, Your Next Level Life*

"Who does he think he is?"

"Oh, he thinks he's all that now!"

"Oh, you too good now?"

Have you ever heard any of these phrases? Too often, when someone in our community reaches financial success, then far too many people have "*something to say.*" Have you ever heard one of these conversations? You might mistakenly believe that someone else's financial gains are literally taking money out of their own pocket.

You know what is at the root of that—a scarcity mentality. We also often call it a "crabs in a barrel" mentality. Stephen Covey, the author of the acclaimed book *Seven Habits of Highly Effective People*, explains that those with a Scarcity Mentality may have an outlook of only a limited amount of pie. If someone gets a slice, that will reduce the pie slice size of others. Individuals with this mindset have a hard time sharing credit or recognition with others, which can translate into not sharing power or profits—including money.

Such a bottom of the barrel mindset not only hampers—but it also cripples one's ability within a community to build wealth. All of us must see ourselves and others as having something worthwhile to contribute. No matter the income level—whether it is sharing a pot of chili or gathering funds for a kid's scholarship—all of us must pitch in. Until we stop seeing some as 'strong' enough to take everyone's requests. Others as too 'helpless' to give. We will continue to drain one group—while failing to empower the other.

Become Crab Proof

I believe that the anecdote to ensure that a scarcity mentality doesn't lodge its presence in your own mindset is to become an impactful giver. The word "impactful" here has significance, especially as it relates to my personal journey. I'll share a couple of personal stories on the topic.

When I was in my twenties, I was fortunate to be a six-figure earner. I felt that I was doing well, purchasing a condo at age 23, and building my emergency savings fund. I could pay all my bills each month, including my credit card debt, student loans, and car note. Because I could go out with friends to nice dinners and readily purchase a nice outfit from a local store, this definitely felt like "arriving" for me after a childhood steeped in poverty.

Yet two incidents challenged my perspective as both shook me to my core. First, one of my family members fell on hard times through no fault of her own. She was evicted from her apartment. She lived in another state and ended up being homeless for a short time. Being one of my favorite people in the world, I found her to be brilliant, industrious, and resilient. Yet I was bothered that I lacked enough financial means to help and pay her first and last month's rent in a new place or even cover her rent for three or four months while she regained her financial footing.

Second, my uncle was diagnosed with brain cancer. As a kid, I always viewed him as a gentle giant as he was a very tall man with a kind, Christ-centered demeanor. When I arrived at his house to spend time with him, I noticed that his showerhead seemed very low, given his height. During his final year here with us, I secretly wanted to sow into his life. I desired to remodel his bathroom with a new showerhead—perhaps one of those cool adjustable ones that would better accommodate him. For all I know, he may have never been bothered by the low showerhead. Yet, I felt deeply disappointed that my financial position at that time prevented me from giving in a way that impacted those I deeply cared for.

After those two incidents, I was motivated to study how people became wealthy, and I discovered it often happened through business ownership. At that point, I immediately started putting a business plan in place. After three years of planning and creating the business infrastructure, I quit my six-figure job. I started my first business motivated by the fact that merely having enough for my four walls was not really enough.

Through many subsequent intentional decisions, including becoming debt-free, we are thankfully now in a position where we can give impactfully. We are intentional givers. Guided with wisdom and discernment, we support family, friends, causes, ministries, and startup businesses. It brings us happiness, for we do so with a joyful heart and open hands.

Finite or Abundant?

When someone views their resources as finite or scarce, many will not engage in this type of joyful and impactful giving. Instead, they will hoard their financial resources to themselves. The few that do give may even see giving as a chore. They often regret every dollar bill that leaves their hands. This has been termed "grudgingly giving." When we allow a biblical worldview to shape us, we can see ourselves as effective conduits. We trust that we are simply tasked with steward-ship—bestowed by our Heavenly Father. We can give with a light heart. Aligned with the biblical principle, "Each of you should give what you have decided in your heart to give, not reluctantly or under compulsion, for God loves a cheerful giver," (II Cor 9:7 NIV).

Give intentionally and joyfully—for that is what God wants. Give to charities. Help out friends or family members. Tithe to churches or ministries. Donate to non-profit organizations. Do something unexpected and thoughtful for a coworker. Whatever approach you choose, the bottom line is that impactful giving is a vital part of a successful financial strategy.

In her book *The Soul of Money*, Lynne Twist describes this transition as moving from a mindset of scarcity to sufficiency. She describes a sufficiency mindset as follows:

> *"When we live in the context of sufficiency, we find a natural freedom and integrity...We feel naturally called to share the resources that flow through our lives – our time, our money, our wisdom, our energy, at whatever level those resources flow – to serve our highest commitments...Sufficiency can be a place to stand, a context that generates a completely new relationship with life, with money, and with everything that money can buy."*

Operating from a sufficiency mindset or impactful giving does not mean you have to support every cause presented to you. You can be prayerful and diligent in your research and still cautious in the ways that you give. That has been our approach, and we would advise you to be thorough and thoughtful in a similar way.

Giving with impact also doesn't always have a high dollar sign next to it. You can buy a work colleague's lunch. Surprise someone with a $10 gift card. Buy an extra uniform at your kid's school for a family in need, or keep snack bags in your car to give to homeless people as my children like to do. The point is to be generous and share the resources that you have. Impactful giving helps you to keep your abundant mindset strong and blessings flowing into your life through the principles of sowing and reaping (II Cor 9:6-10).

Furthermore, it can also help reduce your taxable income! It provides multiple benefits, both internal and external. For this next worksheet, we will identify some of the ways you can start or continue to give impactfully.

Your Habits
Impactful Giving

For the purpose of this exercise, we must separate heart forward impactful giving from soul-draining guilt-driven giving. When we think back to Shawn's story, part of his challenge was that he rarely wanted to spend a lot of time alone. That was why he threw parties at his apartment—at his own expense. That was one of the reasons why he gave freely to his cousins. That's why he ate out as opposed to having dinner at home—alone. That's why he felt guilty about what he had, and others didn't.

You may identify with Shawn's struggles or have your own set of emotional or psychological thought patterns that have impacted the way you view giving through the years. We all have our own experiences that shape us and why we opt *to give* or *not to give*.

So, what emotional pulls commonly motivate us to give out of guilt? Many of our struggles can be summarized in the following statements:

I don't want to be alone or feel unloved.

I don't want to be seen as selfish or rejected.

I may need some help in the future, and this gives me relational credit for that event.

I was never taught that "No" was an option. If you have it—you give it.

This last one may be more challenging to overcome, especially within our community. Many feel kinship, loyalty, and giving go hand in hand. Yet, this desire can become easily misguided when we fail to set healthy boundaries and expectations, as we will discuss in the **Extended Family Impact chapter.**

1. Revisiting the themes in the extended family impact section, are there any re-lationships or connections in your life where you are giving grudgingly or out of guilt? Consider your interactions with people from various parts of your life (i.e., social groups, family members, friends, business partners, or organizations de-manding your time, energy, and money.)

2. To prevent soul-draining, guilt-driven giving in your own life, identify negative thoughts or emotions that motivate you to give. For example, "I don't want to be seen as selfish or rejected." After identifying thoughts or feelings, how can you create boundaries to adjust their impact on your giving decisions?

3. Reread the quote at the beginning of this section. Do you believe that money tru-ly is "plentiful for those who understand the simple laws that govern its acqui-sition?" Or do you think that money and opportunities are finite or only reserved for certain people? Explain why you feel this way.

4. A scarcity mentality can lead to unnecessary competition instead of encouraging and supporting one another. It can also be a sign of an internal fear that you will never have enough and that YOU are never enough. What is/are your greatest fears or worries holding you back from having an abundant mindset? Write them down, read them out loud, then start moving towards replacing these fears with positive thoughts and emotions.

5. Covey explains that those with a scarcity mentality secretly desire to see others suffer some sort of misfortune. If you have been guilty of this, intentionally or unintentionally, take the first step in pivoting your mindset. Write down the name of one person or business you can uplift and a single action you can take within the next week to empower and support them rather than compete.

6. After this week concludes, come back and write what you did and how it made you feel. Set a reminder in your calendar or phone now, so you don't forget.

7. Think, for a moment, about your life's story. At some point, someone gave impactfully to you or your family. Think about that time and write down 5 words that describe how it made you feel. Remember these five words and use it as motivation for the words you want others to feel once you have taken the opportunity to give impactfully.

8. If you had the financial means today, who are the people in your life you would willingly and lovingly support?

9. What situations are your friends or family involved in that could be improved if you were better off financially?

10. On your way to wealth and a debt-free life, one day soon, you will be able to impactfully give more every month to help family, friends, or community needs. List 3–5 specific ways you can be a monthly impactful giver.

11. In light of learning that "grudgingly giving" is a real possibility as well as under-standing 2 Cor 9:7, how can a biblical view of stewardship help transform you into a cheerful giver?

12. You learned that there is no high dollar amount attached to impactful giving. If you are still on your journey to becoming financially comfortable. There are still ways you can be an impactfully give today (i.e., $10 gift cards, buying a col-league lunch, etc.). Name 5 ways you can create a habit of impactful giving now.

Remember, you always have a choice as to who you give to
or where you give.

CHAPTER FIFTEEN

Your Habits
Renting vs. Owning Real Estate

"And we have decided to move into our house because my father - my father - he earned it for us brick by brick...We don't want to make no trouble for nobody or fight no causes, and we will try to be good neighbors. And that's all we got to say about that."

– Walter, A Raisin in the Sun,
  Lorraine Hansberry

The play *A Raisin in the Sun* has resonated with black audiences for decades. From its debut on Broadway in 1959 with Sidney Portier and Ruby Dee to the 2008 movie–remake, featuring Sean Combs, Phylicia Rashad, and Sanaa Lathan. Many themes in the play still remain relevant today. From inheritance in black families often created through death and a life insurance policy to the multi-faceted complexities that black families often face in the pursuit of homeownership. As for the latter, unfortunately, the path to homeownership can still be a complex undertaking for modern black Americans.

Homeownership has historically shown itself to be one of the foundational tenets of wealth accumulation in America. There is a strong correlation between homeownership and higher net worth. In 2019, the Federal Reserve reported that families that own their homes have a median net worth of $255,000 compared to $6,300 for families that rent. However, black Americans cannot simply assume that buying a home will be a default ticket to wealth *for us*. We have to perform additional diligence to ensure the process works as planned.

Why do I say that? Before we discuss developing our wealth habits as it relates to real estate. Let's take a moment to dissect some opportunities and barriers black Americans regularly face—specifically related to achieving the often-touted American dream of homeownership.

Homeownership can be deeply personal. Many of us have internalized that nothing says wealth more in the US than having your own home. However, books like *The Color of Law* by Richard Rothstein point out how black WWII veterans did not gain the appreciation of home equity. The reason was that, unfortunately, discrimination persisted in the mortgage and lending practices. What is even worse is that it happened under US policy. The Joint Center for Political and Economic Studies explains how the wealth gap continued post–World War II. It was during this period when the US had its first major homeownership growth activity. This is powerful because such growth has led some to conclude that wealth transfer via homeownership has hardly been realized for African Americans. If we want to generate wealth via homeownership, we have to do our homework. We have to take the extra steps to understand what we are signing up for.

That Pesky Wage Gap

First, the wage gap has created an obstacle to homeownership. "With higher unemployment rates and less wealth, to begin with, black Americans were less able to buy homes even when prices were at their lowest point, meaning many missed out on opportunities to build wealth and put down roots in their communities through homeownership," said Redfin chief economist Daryl Fairweather.

This, in turn, has led many of us to settle for renting homes or apartments to fill the gap. African-American households tend to be overwhelmingly renters," said Ralph McLaughlin, deputy chief economist at CoreLogic. "When you couple a shortage of homes on the owner-occupancy side with a rental market that up until now has been pretty robust, it makes it very difficult to save for a down payment if your rents are going up faster than your incomes." If recent trends continue, an

Urban Institute report states that black Americans born between 1965–1975 "will likely become part of the first generation since those born before 1900 to reach retirement age with more renters than homeowners among their community."

This macro-level trend has created a predominant landscape around many of us, where the norm we see is often renting. For some, that socialization creates the need for a mindset shift that owning a house is something that we can and, in many cases, should do to advance our financial futures.

The tough thing about referencing these macro-level statistics is that I know this mental or environmental challenge regarding renting versus owning is not everyone's reality. I have aunts and uncles and cousins who own their own homes, and I'm sure you have those too. You may have grown up with parents that own and grandparents that own. I love the diversity of our economic experiences. Adopting the belief that homeownership is attainable may not be a mindset challenge for all of us. Still, it can be a hurdle for some.

Do You Have It All Together?

Once you determine that homeownership is a route you want to take, then most will need to take out a loan specifically for housing called a mortgage. There are numerous financial steps you must take to qualify for a mortgage. One of the first steps is ensuring that your credit is in decent and ideally good or excellent shape. At a minimum, your credit score needs to be at least 580 to qualify for a mortgage loan.

You will also need to ensure the consumer debt you have is low. Mortgage underwriters will look at your debt-to-income ratio. They want to ensure your monthly debt payments do not impede your ability to pay the monthly mortgage payment. After addressing your credit. or as you are in the process of doing so, depending on your cash flow, you will also need to ensure you save intentionally for a down payment. You should also identify programs that can provide additional down payment assistance. There are numerous federal, state, and local programs available.

Mortgage loans such as those offered through the Federal Housing Administration (FHA) can make the path to homeownership easier for first-time buyers.

After getting all these items in order, you will want to find a mortgage company that will issue you a loan. From there, it is best to find a realtor to work with on your home search and purchase process since they know the ins and outs of property in any particular area.

However, even with all of your ducks in a row, *you* could still be denied. According to a 2018 Lending Tree study, black Americans had the highest *denial* rates for mortgages at 17.4 percent. white Americans, on the other hand, had the lowest denial rate at 7.9 percent. Yet even when black Americans secure the loan, there is another hurdle right in front of us.

Many headlines feature stories where national banks purposely raised interest rates for black applicants. This is not merely a historical fact but one that unfortunately remains recent and persistent. For example, researchers at the University of California Berkeley analyzed nearly 7 million 30-year mortgages. Their findings suggest lenders charged black and Latino applicants higher interest rates. The average was almost .08 percent, and the refinancing fees were higher for blacks and Latinos than white Americans.

The same Berkeley study reported that 1.3 million creditworthy black and Latino applicants were rejected from mortgages. Researchers stated that if ethnicity was not a factor, those applicants would have been accepted. *How do you know that to be true, you ask?* Because when racial or ethnic identifiers were removed from applications, the mortgages *were approved*.

To Buy or Not to Buy?

Does this mean you shouldn't buy a house or buy a home by using a mortgage loan? Of course not! But you can't fight a battle you don't know is there. How do you conquer this battle?

- Go into the process with eyes wide open.
- Identify competitive mortgage interest rates for your credit and income profile.
- Get estimates from multiple lenders.
- Compare one lender to the next.
- Negotiate to ensure you are getting an excellent rate.

The higher your credit score, salary, savings, and income from additional streams — the more leverage you will have. So, it's not one-sided—you have to also do your part.

For your mortgage broker or mortgage lender selection process, do your research on the lending institutions you are interested in working with. Ask your friends and family for recommendations for mortgage lenders they have worked with and received impressive results. Many of us may think of shopping around for a good deal on a car or furniture—comparing prices at different car lots or furniture stores. Shopping for a mortgage is no different. You can create the power to negotiate favorable terms that align with your goal of building wealth.

One of the best pieces of advice I ever received about preparing for a successful relationship was to spend more time preparing for the actual marriage than I did the wedding. For black Americans, we have to do the same thing with the home buying process. We need to spend as much time preparing and understanding the mortgage we will take on as we do to identify the actual house.

We cannot choose to be ignorant of the details. Especially not while signing the paperwork for the most significant financial decision most of us will ever make in our lifetime.

- Read the fine print.
- Ask questions.
- Understand the repayment terms, the amortization tables, the total cost of the mortgage over time.
- Know how discount points work.
- Ensure you are clear on every item listed on your pre-approval and other term sheets.
- Conduct internet searches for terms you don't understand.
- Empower yourself with the knowledge to make an informed decision about the mortgage loan product you use—not just the house you purchase.

Know Your Why

Now, let's talk about the actual house. When it comes time to purchase a home—you should understand what strategic benefit you want the house to serve. Why are you buying a home? After experiencing multiple apartment evictions during my childhood, homeownership has an emotionally deep tie to stability, not just wealth accumulation for me. What is *your* reason?

- Do you want to live near family and friends?

- Do you want great schools?

- Are you buying this home because you want to pass it down to your children?

- Are you buying it as a status symbol?

- Are you buying this home solely as a wealth-generating strategy?

It is a *home*—so while it *can* build wealth, there may be multiple reasons you may buy one. The reason behind me bringing this up is that you must be thoughtful about where you purchase and the types of home you plan to purchase so that those attributes align with your desired outcomes.

Also, know and plan for the tax implications of homeownership. This is key as many minority-owned homes continue to be assessed at higher tax rates than homes owned by white Americans. This idea was discussed in a working paper by Carlos Avenancio-Leo of Indiana University and Troup Howard of the University of Utah. Both economists looked at more than a decade of tax assessment and sales data for 118 million homes in the US Their introduction included this overview:

> *Within US Census block groups, which represent regions of approximately 1,200 people, an average minority homeowner has an assessment 5–6% higher relative to market price than her nonminority neighbor. This latter finding is particularly surprising given that most assessors likely neither know, nor observe, homeowner race. We document that a significant portion of this effect arises from racial differentials in assessment appeals. To do so, we first analyze appeals in Cook County, the second largest county in the US Using administrative court records, we show that minority homeowners: (i) are less likely to appeal their assessment, (ii)*

conditional on appealing, are also less likely to win, and(iii) conditional on success, typically receive a smaller reduction than nonminority residents. Then we show that national assessment patterns around changes in racial ownership follow this channel: within the same property, assessment growth is significantly higher during the tenure of a black or Hispanic homeowner.

As a homeowner, you also should gain a clear understanding of the tax assessment trends in the neighborhood you intend to buy in and familiarize yourself with the assessment appeals process.

Applied Knowledge Is Powerful

- Should black Americans be denied homeownership despite creditworthiness?

- Should the same mortgage products cost us more simply because of our ethnicity?

- Should we pay more in property taxes due to our minority status?

Of course not! We know there is policy and structural work to be done. Thankfully, we do have advocates and non-profits such as the Center for Responsible Lending—taking on those causes to dismantle these unfair discriminatory housing and mortgage-lending practices.

On a micro-level today, before we jump headfirst into a perfect ideal such as homeownership, we must first identify all the pieces of the puzzle uniquely impacting us. Take the time to understand the mortgage product you agree to. Conduct the research on the banking institution you are receiving it from and make an informed decision in alignment with your personal goals about what house you buy.

If we are not intentional and knowledgeable, then we may mistake the act of taking on a mortgage for a home as an award. When, in reality, it can become a penalty if we don't arm ourselves with the proper knowledge and apply it to our process.

Keep Your Options Open

That is *if* you choose to buy a home. Y'all may be noticing my trend here. **It's about options.** While a well-informed decision regarding homeownership can be a key component in your strategy to attain a #7-Figure Net Worth and beyond, there are also other paths. Every generation does see real estate differently. I notice that the modern landscape is shifting across ethnicities, and the default to homeownership is something that many millennials and gen z Americans are challenging.

So, if traditional homeownership is not something you want to participate in, there is still a hands-off approach available. Instead, you may opt to participate in the housing market through a Real Estate Investment Trust (REIT), which is a type of investment we will discuss more in the **Investing** chapter.

Listen. However, you slice it, the fact will remain that what you pay to cover your four walls will likely be one of your highest expenses throughout your life. Therefore, it is essential to have a clear strategy regarding how you want to allocate that expense in your pursuit of wealth. Plan. Research that plan. Improve that plan and then go execute it!

Current Homeowners

Do you own your home, or are you about to close on a house? There are strategies you can apply to accelerate your use of homeownership as a wealth-building tool.

HELOC Accelerated Payoff Strategy

There are few things more satisfying for a homeowner than approaching the end of your mortgage loan, especially when it is right around the corner. What if there is a way to get to that moment quicker? Strategically leveraging a home equity line of credit (HELOC) is a way to boost you to that final mortgage payment. Now, it will take a lot of discipline to pull this off, but it is possible. The first thing you will need is a positive cash flow—which is when your monthly income exceeds your expenses. Second, you need a credit card that will essentially give you a grace period.

From there, it becomes a balancing act between applying a full month's pay-check to your mortgage while using your credit card to pay off the rest of your monthly expenses. If I dive into the details here, this will turn into a senior thesis. Fortunately, many websites can give you a better idea of how to leverage a HELOC to pay off your mortgage early. I would search Amazon for books or YouTube for videos that delve deeper into this topic. This may not be an approach for everyone. Still, it could be a very savvy strategy if you determine, with the accountability and help of a financial coach, that this could work for you.

Payment Terms

Grab your mortgage papers. Call your financial institution and see if you can change your payment terms to every two weeks instead of one monthly payment. The idea here is to get in an extra payment each year, which will help pay down your balance quicker. You may also want to identify other ways to make additional payments towards your principal above the minimum required.

Mortgage Terms

Check out the terms on your mortgage. Are you in an adjustable-rate prod-uct with a balloon payment coming up? Do you have equity in your home with a high-interest rate product compared to current market rates? If so, you may want to consider refinancing. If you refinance, consider keeping the focus on lowering your interest rate and not readjusting your monthly payment. For example, if you are 15 years into a 30-year mortgage, consider refinancing to a 15-year product and not resetting the amortization table with another 30-year mortgage. If your budget can tolerate the same payment amount. After refinancing to a lower inter-est rate, you can contribute more to the principal each month and accelerate your payoff time by keeping your payment the same. Take some time to research refi-nancing, talk to multiple lenders, and see if refinancing is the right move for you.

Now, let's take a moment to explore your plans related to homeownership with this next worksheet.

Your Habits

Renting vs. Owning Real Estate

1. Do you currently own your own home? If so, are you satisfied with your purchase? Why or why not?

2. If you are a homeowner, did you feel you were well-informed and educated about the process? Were you aware of the history of unfair lending practices for black and Latino buyers before making your purchase?

3. Do you agree that homeownership is a foundational part of the wealth creation process? If so, in light of this chapter, do you believe this is true for black Americans as well?

For current homeowners . . .

4. For homeowners, review the terms of your current mortgage. On a scale of 1–10, how would you rank the terms? Why did you rate it this way?

5. Is there anything about your mortgage you don't fully understand? Write down 3 steps you will take in the next 30 days to better understand your current mortgage.

6. Do you know the total cost of your mortgage once fully amortized? If so, what will it be?

7. What, if any changes, do you need to make regarding your current mortgage product?

8. Do you want to buy additional personal real estate (vacation homes, etc.)?

9. If so, research the types of properties (doesn't have to be the specific property just yet) and evaluate your current finances as a whole. After doing this, determine 3 steps you can take in the next 3 months to advance that goal of acquiring additional personal property?

For future homeowners . . .

10. What is your current motivation to purchase a home? Write this down and read it frequently as a reminder to keep making positive moves towards this goal.

11. What type of mortgage product do you plan to use to buy a home? Why have you chosen this as your best option?

12. What are your top five financial institutions that you are interested in receiving your mortgage from? Why?

13. Evaluate your current financial responsibilities and your financial goals. Taking these figures into account: 1) What price range of house can you afford? 2) What monthly mortgage payment can you afford?

14. Do you have funds saved for a down payment? If no, how much do you have saved? How much more do you need to accumulate? (You will need to know the type of mortgage you want and your home's estimated cost to get a more precise amount.)

15. Now that you know the amount remaining that you need to save toward your down payment, write down your action plan (the steps you need and are willing to take to achieve this goal). Just as important, give yourself a deadline to reach this financial goal.

16. As part of your plan, research and write down each local, state, and federal down payment assistance or first-time home buyer program you could qualify for.

17. Which ones will you apply for, and by what date?

18. What is the name of your real estate agent?

If you do not have one yet, ask friends and families who are homeowners and conduct online research. Narrow your list down to at least three agents who meet your personal qualifications. Then interview all three to decide which one is the best fit for your homeownership journey.

If you are opting away from traditional homeownership . . .

19. Do you plan to integrate real estate into your wealth-building strategy? Why or why not?

20. Will you invest in REITs?

21. If yes, have you begun to research your options? Which ones interest you the most? Why?

22. If not for personal use, will you buy real estate for investment purposes (rentals, buy and flip, etc.)?

CHAPTER SIXTEEN

Your Habits
Assembling Your Financial Squad

"Where there is no counsel, the people fall; But in the multitude of counselors there is safety."

– Proverbs 11:14 (New King James Version)

Whenever you are working towards a goal, you must have a team of people providing wise counsel and supporting your goals. A key part of the #7–Figure Net Worth blueprint is assembling your own squad of wise counsel—the financial experts, supporters, and friends around you—that can help you reach your goal.

1. Accountability Partners

When it comes to reaching your goals, you are far more likely to reach your goal if you have a plan for accountability in place. Results from a study on accountability performed by the American Society of Training and Development reported that you will have a 65% likelihood of reaching a goal if you create accountability with someone. Want to increase that likelihood to 95%? The study shared that having a consistent appointment to check in with that person will increase your chances of success.

The changes that we are talking about in this book are not always easy—it requires changing our mindsets and daily habits. So one of the first steps you will want to take is to find a friend or two to hold you accountable. This should be somebody that you are willing to be totally honest with about your finances and that you give the right to "check" you whenever you're shopping a little too much or getting lax on your monthly reconciliation. There are few things sweeter than achieving a goal with your friends, especially when it comes to financial freedom. If you don't have anyone in your circle yet, feel free to connect with someone in our #7-Figure Net Worth Facebook group or even use your financial coach as your accountability partner as well.

2. Community

Like the power of having accountability, there is tremendous impact with being plugged into a larger community of like-minded individuals with similar goals of financial freedom and creating generational wealth. It is powerful to be connected to a strong group of people to encourage, give advice, and feedback on your financial decisions. The black community's strength is amazing, and for that, you need to look no further than Black Wall Street. Many of us are familiar with Tulsa, Oklahoma's community, bombed by white terrorists in 1921. They built doctor's offices, schools, and other programs designed to strengthen the black community. It is unfortunate that Black Wall Street had to face a traumatic end like that, but who is to say that we aren't the next generation to create something like that? A strong black community can positively affect our future, and it can quite possibly start with you.

So while you may not start with redeveloping tracts of land to create a hub of financial empowerment (although I would totally be here for it), you can start by perhaps starting a book club, a class at church or just a monthly check-in virtually or in-person with a group of friends. You may also decide to plug into an existing community like a group coaching program or an investment club. Regardless of what it looks like in your life, be intentional to plug into or create a community focused on wealth around you to help you maintain and accelerate your progress towards reaching and exceeding your financial goals.

3. Financial Coach and Financial Advisors

Y'all remember the movie *A Thin Line Between Love and Hate*? Martin Lawrence and Lynn Whitefield showed us that there is a thin line between those two. I'm going to share a different thin line with you now. In the financial world, there is a thin but significant line between a financial advisor and a financial coach. So much so that the line is often blurred between the two.

The problem with that is that historical minimums for working with financial advisors have left many black Americans believing that we have to be at a certain income or asset level before we need to work with any type of financial expert— and that could not be further from the truth. Most black Americans could significantly benefit from working with a financial coach today, even if they may not yet be in a position to need a financial advisor. Learning the difference between the two can be a financial game-changer.

A Comparison

A clear way to draw a line between the two is that financial advisors manage and build the wealth you have already accumulated. In contrast, financial coaches help you to initially create wealth. In a blog explaining the growing financial coaching industry, Garret Philbin, a financial coach, explained the difference between a financial coach and a financial advisor.

> *"Financial advisors tend to focus on implementing financial products and strategies, while financial coaches focus more on the basics of personal money management, behavioral change, and accountability to a client-driven spending plan. And while financial advisors most commonly help to manage the wealth that already exists, a financial coach's job is to provide a client the knowledge, skills, and behaviors that will help them build wealth in the first place."*

The Coach

Essentially, a financial coach can help you with the come up, and a financial advisor can help keep you there. Aside from the ways their roles differ, a financial coach and financial advisor also differ in their qualifications, how they work with their client, and their cost.

Financial coaching is an industry that is fairly new and is experiencing a lot of growth. Philbin shares a few other labels that you may hear that also identify a "financial coach" like money coach, financial life coach, certified money coach, etc. These all fall under the same umbrella. The same shirt style with a different name brand—a polo is still a polo, and a coach is still a coach. The title doesn't matter as much as the main objective.

A great financial coach will encourage you to continually learn about finance, challenge you to step up and take responsibility for your financial actions, and can also be a source of accountability in your journey. They will help you get a clear plan of where you currently are and design a path for where you aspire to financially go.

Think of a college basketball superstar on the verge of being drafted into the NBA. His college coach knows that he is headed in the right direction. Still, a great coach will continue to help him obtain the necessary knowledge and skills to maintain high performance at the next level. A financial coach does much of the same.

This person will help you understand the basics of personal finance and help you develop and maintain healthy financial habits. Their main job is to empower their clients to reach their financial goals and learn how to handle their finances responsibly. On average, financial coaching can cost anywhere from $40–$600 per one-hour session. However, financial advisors bring a different set of skills.

The Advisor

Philbin further explains, "financial advisors help clients reach financial goals by recommending how to allocate and invest the client's money. For many, those goals include a comfortable retirement and perhaps education funds for children, but goals might also be pursuing a second career, buying a vacation home, or starting a business."

Financial advisors are usually sought when you have accumulated enough money and/or assets, and you want it effectively managed. There are two common payment structures for financial advisors: fee-only and commission-based.

Fee-only

These advisors provide financial help for a fee. The fee may be an hourly rate session fee. It may be charged as an annual percentage of assets under management (common among investment advisors). Financial advisors can help you with wealth management, financial and family planning, investment strategies, and more. Some financial advisors can also help you with budgeting and debt reduction—which is one area that their services can overlap with a financial coach. In this payment structure, you will be told the fee for each service or session initially.

Commission-based

Commission-based financial advisors may offer the same services as fee-only advisors but are compensated differently. For some products or services, they may receive a commission from fund companies or brokerages for financial product sales. For other services, they may charge a percentage of the total amount that their clients invest in for particular funds or products.

Fee- and commission-based

Some advisors may offer a combination of the two. The advisor charges a flat fee and earns a commission on the investments that you purchase.

Regardless of the fee structure offered, it's important that you understand the compensation upfront and then make an informed decision about which fee structure and respective advisor best fits your personal financial goals. You can even work with your financial coach to help identify the type of advisor and associated compensation structure that would be the best fit for you.

4. CPA/Tax Advisor

As your income grows, one of the biggest challenges you will face is our Uncle Sam showing up with his hand out. As soon as you get money rolling in, our dear old Unc will expect you to give him his due, and at some point, that may mean making additional payments every quarter.

As your income grows and your tax brackets climb, Unc will become more and more visible. So it is important early on to begin to integrate tax-advantaged strategies into your financial plan. The keyword here is tax-advantaged, *not* tax evasive. We've seen Wesley Snipes face prison time for tax evasion, so trust me, that's not what you want. But there are many legal ways to loosen the stranglehold that Uncle Sam may try to get on your finances.

Your first step will be to speak with a tax advisor to discuss the best tax reduction strategies to implement based on your situation. A tax advisor is an expert who has specialized training and education in tax accounting and tax law. This type of advisor can help you minimize your tax burden while ensuring you are compliant with all current laws. They can help you identify deductions that you can achieve through government programs, employer benefits, family and child credits, business write-offs, and charitable contributions as examples. Note that this is not just your tax preparer. Not all tax preparers have obtained these additional qualifications to become an enrolled tax agent or a certified public accountant (CPA). However, there are many tax agents and CPAs that also prepare taxes. You'll just want to ask them about their credentials and proceed accordingly.

Family and Child Credits

Um so, before I get into the details of this credit. Just one question—can we please stop claiming other people's kids on our income tax? I know we may be looking for every avenue to save funds, but if the IRS ever decides to audit you, you'll be asking if that extra money was really worth it. However, under current guidelines, the child tax credit for *your child(ren)* will provide you a credit of up to $2,000 per child under the age of 17. If the credit exceeds taxes owed, families may receive up to $1,400 per child as a refund. Just something to think about!

Beyond the Baseline

As your income increases and you accumulate a higher value of accumulating assets, the type of tax-advantaged strategies you discuss with your tax advisor will begin to diversify and evolve into what I call intermediate tax strategies. Two examples of such strategies are angel investments and charitable remainder trusts.

Angel Investments

Whether you begin angel investing because you love entrepreneurship and business ventures or are consistently approached by friends and family looking for startup capital—if leveraged strategically, that invested money could help you with your tax bill.

The United States Government truly wants its citizens to start more businesses. So much so that they have provided cushions and benefits to startup companies that also extends to those that invest in the startup. From an immediate write off of up to 25 percent of your investment to receiving tax breaks that allow investors to take up to 100 percent of their capital gains tax-free, under current guidelines, angel investing is a good way to provide more of a shield from Uncle Sam when tax time rolls around.

To receive this deduction, you will need to meet the IRS guidelines to be considered an accredited investor. For 2020, those income guidelines meant those who were filing individually needed a reported income of $200,000 or more in the most recent two years or more than $300,000 if filing jointly with a spouse in that same period. You can also qualify if you have at least $1 million in investable assets, excluding the value of the home that you live in.

Charitable Remainder Trust

A charitable remainder trust is a hybrid or "split-interest" vehicle that allows you to create a potential income stream by donating to a trust while also contributing to a charitable organization that you choose. You can accomplish this through this tax-exempt, irrevocable trust designed to help you reduce the amount of taxes you are liable for. This is a great strategy to employ when you are looking for asset diversification and tax-advantaged options.

Designing a charitable remainder trust can be intricate. The IRS has guidelines about the percentages that the annuity can provide in relation to the trust assets.

So you would likely want to employ the help of both a tax and financial advisor when adding this to your financial portfolio.

Now that we understand the different profiles, with this next worksheet, let's talk about what professionals should be on your personal roster today, within the next year, and beyond.

Your Habits

Assembling Your Financial Squad

....

1. If you have never taken the time to seek a financial coach or advisor, what has held you back? The idea that you don't have enough money yet? Worried about the cost? Worried about being taken advantage of or cheated? Another reason? Whatever your reason(s), write it down below.

2. If your answer to question one was no longer an issue for you, and you decided to hire financial expertise, what is the first topic you would seek guidance on?

3. In what way do you believe a financial coach can best help you? Personal money management, behavior change, accountability, etc.? What do you believe you can improve about that area(s)?

4. In what area of your finances are you least confident in your current knowledge?

5. What are 3 financial goals you believe that you could achieve with the help of a financial coach?

6. What are 3 emotional benefits you believe you could achieve through working with a financial coach?

7. We learned that a financial advisor helps to manage your wealth with proven products and strategies. What are 3 wealth goals you believe you can achieve with the help of a financial advisor?

8. Describe your perfect retirement. Be specific about what you are doing daily, how old you are, and what your monthly expenses consist of. After learning about a financial advisor's function, do you think you can reach that dream retirement scenario on your own, or would you benefit from bringing an advisor into the equation?

9. Decide whether a financial coach or financial advisor is best for your current financial situation. Next, research options locally and online. Once you narrow down your options, write down the names of your top three choices, your con-sultation date/time, and then come back and note your key takeaways from each of your consultations.

CHAPTER SEVENTEEN

Your Habits
Investing

> *"Black millionaires repeatedly take certain actions, consistently adhering to routines that allow them to create and maintain considerable wealth. They save, dream, plan, invest, and give in a never-ending cycle. Behind their routines and habits lies a basic core of beliefs - the first of which is that money is plentiful for those who understand the simple laws that govern its acquisition."*
>
> *– Dennis Kimbro, Author, The Wealth Choice, Success Secrets of Black Millionaires*

You may have heard the song, "I got five on it." When it comes to that five, we should have a little more on it than that! Regarding what Luniz spoke of—our 'it' will be something different. Our 'it' will be investments that can raise our net worth.

Investments are pivotal as a person shifts from financial management tools of solely checking and savings accounts to net worth statements and personal balance sheets. As your financial savvy increases, you will also learn to create, structure, and manage investment portfolios. As you develop your investment portfolios, it can become one of the most prominent aspects of your net worth and the foundation for establishing generational wealth. While black Americans have, in the past, been hesitant about investing, especially in the stock market, that trend is changing.

Black Millennials Are About That Investment Life

Many black millennials are catching on to the importance of investing. Ariel Investments recently conducted research showing that 67 percent of black Americans under 40 earning at least $50,000 annually are investing in stocks directly or through mutual funds. While our white counterparts' investment rate is still higher, at 73 percent, that difference averaging at 7% between black Americans and white Americans millennials of 7 percentage points is the smallest of all the age brackets for participants.

Translation, progress alert! The wealth gap is tiniest among black millennials and their counterparts, which shows some serious gains. So, yay for us! It appears that black millennials are on the right track to prepare for generational wealth. The Ariel Investments study also revealed that 41 percent of black Americans say the stock market is the best investment, increasing from 28 percent in 2004.

Many of us are downloading apps, reading books, calling our advisors about our 401(k)s or alternative retirement funds, and taking the leap! Hooray! As our funds move full steam in our chosen investment vehicles, we strive towards a brighter future. One area we must be particularly intentional about investing in as black Americans is our retirement. One of the top reasons that many of us are in a position where we need to provide financial support to our parents is because they did not have the funds, resources, or education to properly prepare for their retirement.

While it genuinely brings me joy to provide financial support to my mom during her retirement years, it is not something I expect or want my children to do for us when we retire. By being thoughtful and goal-oriented in the way we invest for retirement now, we are lightening the impact that the "black tax" may have on our own children. It is up to us individually and collectively to reach our goals, become exceptional at our financial game, and set a table of success for the next generation.

Taking the Leap

I'm taking the leap and doing it—and I feel the least qualified to do so. However, sometimes all it takes is a little courage to take those first steps. While I do not consider myself an investment maven because I am absolutely still learning, I have spent the past decade with my spouse listening to those teaching various levels of investment strategies. From podcasts to YouTube videos, I aim to educate myself as much as possible. My husband has joined investment groups. As a couple, we have had many conversations with our financial coach and friends about investment-related topics we hear or read about. We have been intentional about making investing an integrated part of our life.

By doing this, I intentionally decided to crush my stagnant mindset and push past poverty-induced thinking to make my financial journey—a self-taught university. I have consistently pushed myself toward learning and acquiring more financial acumen. So has my husband. With every financial article we read that we don't fully understand at first, and every annual or monthly investment account statement that we carefully review, we sharpen our financial acumen.

In case you didn't quite catch that. Let me say it *again* for those in the back— **please open your investment account statements and actually read each one of them.** If you happen to be one of those millennials with your duckets (random fact – from the Italian word 'ducat,' meaning gold coins) planted and growing in investments, please take the time to understand the terms and each line item in your investment account statements, so you have a sense of the process of how money grows. For all of us, *understanding and tracking* the vehicles we put our money in must become *just as important* as growing our funds.

Hanging Out on the Sidelines

While many of us are jumping in, we have all heard our fair share of stories or been involved in conversations with mid-to-high income earners with beautiful melanin skin sitting out on the investment sidelines—even leaving the matched funds for 401(k)s left untouched. Which, um, is one of the closest things to gaining free money. You may have even heard of checking accounts with huge sums earning next to nothing in interest. A key financial tenet is that wherever you stack your cash, you want to ensure that your savings or investment accounts, at the very least, are growing with interest rates that surpass inflation. This is where using money market accounts can be a highly strategic option.

When someone you know or an article you read recommends moving your funds from a savings account to a money market account, the idea can initially be challenging. Especially if all you have ever known is savings accounts. However, making moves like this are critical to just keeping pace with the changing world around us. According to financial advisors at Investopedia, money market accounts beat inflation, thus preserving our future buying power. Instead of running away from investments, we should be embracing them.

Let's face it, though. While all of this may sound good at face value, for many of us, it has been a completely different upbringing with these money things. For example, Lazetta Rainey Braxton, CFP and founder of Financial Fountains, said that historically in the black community, there have been fewer conversations in the home about investing. "I've found that my white millennial (clients) have had more dinner table conversations about (wealth-building)," Braxton said. "There just has been more wealth in their lives, and they have more (comfort) with investing."

The numbers clearly show (and while we know there are exceptions in our community for which we are grateful), a lack of discretionary income for black Americans has been problematic. For example, a Brookings Institute study found that black Americans hold 1/10 of the net worth of white families in the US Many black families are financially vulnerable and less likely to discuss something that is not as prevalent in their lives—investing discretionary income.

If you are reading this today and hanging out on the investments sideline is your current situation—no shade. I hope this insight provides you with the motivation you need to invest. To make a true dent in the wealth gap, more African Americans must get into the investment game. That means *you* too! Investing, however, like any other financial behavior, is tied to a mindset. For many of us, we have been taught, socialized, and conditioned in pockets of black society to either hold money too tightly (under a mattress)—or spend funds too freely (standing in the line for the new J's as soon as payday hits). Let us consider a few examples.

Because of the Great Depression in the 1930s, destabilizing bank runs were common. After those experiences, many of our elders feared losing money and never trusted the banks again. For example, I have a friend whose grandmother lived during the Great Depression. Her grandmother was an avid saver. While she did have a savings account—she always kept some of her most valuable things throughout her home in things like bags and recycled cans because she never wanted to be without again.

Similarly, many African Americans in times past felt distrustful of banks due to a lot of the shadiness that took place historically. In many cases, this distrust of financial institutions has passed down into modern times, and money hiding still happens. Money is still being tucked away under a mattress, not earning any interest. Some may be tucking away funds in a savings account (not for an emergency per se) and not taking advantage of better-earned interest in a money market account, simply because they fear any investment offering any level of risk.

We often hold on to money tightly because fear influences our financial decisions. As if history was not enough, the most recent Great Recession exacerbated many African Americans' fears similar to those in the Great Depression. For example, during that period, the unemployment rate was twice as high for black Americans than white Americans.

Stock the Cash

Some may still be on the investment sidelines simply due to a lack of knowledge or understanding. To quote professional NBA player Kobe Bryant, "The stock market is the same animal and a different beast." In a humorous response, Kanye West asked, "What the **fudge** does that mean, Kobe?" Well, at least Kanye had the gusto to ask. I will try to explain Kobe's metaphor. There are so many levels to stocks—stocks with dividends, growth stocks, defensive stocks, and so forth. It is not something that you will easily understand in a day. It will take time and intentionality. Now a billionaire, Warren Buffett, did not reach his level of wealth overnight—he was 11 years old when he started investing.

That same potential to grow our portfolios to a significant amount over time remains available to us. It just takes a bit of commitment to educating ourselves, time (*a key factor in compound interest*), patience, and a disciplined and consistent investment strategy. Often investing is not something you can jump into, throw money at, and hope it lands sweetly. You need to know how and where to invest. For example, Eszylfie Taylor, founder of Taylor Insurance and Financial Services, advises us to:

> *"Invest early and often. No one (truly) knows when the market is at its height or low, so a well-balanced, diversified, long-term approach is advisable. Understand your risk tolerance, time horizon, and investment options. The best plans for short-term liquidity and access to cash are typically the worst plans for long-term growth and income. Conversely, the best plans for long-term growth and income are typically the worst plans for short term liquidity and access to cash."*

If the stock market is the focus of your next financial move, recognize you do not have to take the plunge into the stock market alone. Consider taking investment classes, hiring a certified financial planner (CFP) or financial advisor, or joining an investment club. Many of the investment retirement programs offered through employers include complimentary sessions with investment advisors. The design of your investment strategy will be unique to your income, circumstances, and goals, whether in the stock market or any other financial arena. There is an abundance of information available online—and apps like Robin Hood can also provide you with interesting investment opportunities and ideas.

Once you get started or grow your portfolio, take the time to identify the good investments, including learning which stocks, bonds, and mutual funds best fit your individual financial blueprint. If you are a frequent customer at a store, research the company's financial performance and find pricing on its stock. If you want to invest in a few shares, go for it, and move up from there. For example, I did exactly as I have described with a store where I often shop. Since I enjoy its product lines and trust its brand, I did not mind investing funds in their stock. Similarly, you can invest in a few shares of a brand that you know and trust to help you start.

As previously mentioned, you can also accumulate wealth by getting involved in real estate investing through REITs. As previously mentioned, you can also accumulate wealth by getting involved in real estate investing through REITs. A REIT functions by owning, operating, or financing real estate properties that generate income. They are modeled after mutual funds – pooling the capital of multiple investors. This makes it possible for individual investors to earn dividends from real estate investments without buying, managing, or financing any properties directly. Numerous REITs are publicly traded on major securities exchanges. Investors can buy and sell them in a similar manner as stocks throughout the trading season.

Investments can also be made in art, annuities, and cryptocurrency (although some advisors are wary of this type of investment—so do your homework). One of the most common places to start investing, if employed, is your 401(k). If you are self-employed or have maxed out your 401(k) contributions, you may also consider investing through an independent retirement account (IRA).

What's Your Hang-Up?

For those who may have not yet leaped into investing, what are your hang-ups with doing so? Is it the fear of losing investments? Is it a concern that you lack the financial acumen to choose a sound investment? Whatever it is—we must deal with our mindsets, emotions, and grow our knowledge base so that they do not keep us from investing.

Perhaps, start by reading one financial resource that supplies sound education and investment advice. It could be Forbes, Business Insider, the Economist, or even a magazine covering FinTech (i.e., financial technology). You could save up and attend one community college or enroll in online courses to strengthen your knowledge. Your first step may just be to start a conversation with someone in your life who is knowledgeable and trustworthy with investing.

If you are pushing just to make ends meet and cannot invest at this time—that is okay. Because this blueprint helps you reach that point. I still want you to prepare your mind now—so that when that time comes, you will be more likely to invest in the right financial engines and spend less on the wrong ones. We know that extra money can come in many forms. Bonuses, raises, extra income, and yet you must grasp financial knowledge as fast as you obtain the funds so you can immediately apply your understanding to improve your situation.

Regardless of where or when you start, I emphasize making it a priority to begin or continue investing. While it is important to make money, it is far better for money to grow and serve you. Strategic investing is one of the key components of creating generational wealth and an important part in closing the wealth gap.

You now have the choice to allow your finances to work in a manner that outpaces inflation and taxes or to hold it tightly and know it is all you will ever have. I encourage the first choice—initiate, grow, or expand your knowledge about investing through resources that surround you, and then just do it! As an investor, you are money's master—not its servant. It is your choice—your money can either work hard for you, or you will always work hard for it. So figure it out and find a way to put more than "five" into your investments.

Take Action!

Identify and integrate at least one resource that can shift your mindset in investing. **What is one resource concerning investing that you can integrate into your life daily, weekly, or monthly?** It could be a library book or an Audible download, a podcast or YouTube video series, an online magazine, or articles.

Find Us on Facebook

Once you identify at least one, share the investing resource(s) that you will use in our #7 Figure Net Worth Facebook group.

For me, I chose the investing channel on the Flipboard app. Even though I do not always understand all the terms, I force myself to read the articles. Over time, the articles have started making more sense to me. So, push past your comfort zone and find a resource to upgrade your investing knowledge!

WORKSHEET

Your Habits
Investing
....

1. Again, here are the findings from Ariel Investment's study: 67% of black Americans under 40 with at least $50K invest in stocks. If you fall into this age and money category, are you a part of the 67% who invest or the 33% who do not?

2. If you are a part of the 67%, how has investing benefited you?

3. If you are a part of the 33%, what is holding you back from investing?

If you are currently investing

4. Do you regularly read through your investment account statements, or have you been happy merely knowing you invest?

If you are one of those happy investors or you read through but admittedly don't understand all of what you read, I need you to do this now:

- *Open your most recent account statement.*

- *Grab a pen or open the note-taking application on your phone.*

- *As you read, note or highlight anything you do not understand.*

- *Next, search online, talk to a knowledgeable friend, or call the company to learn how to confidently read and understand your investment statements.*

5. Are you interested in taking your investing acumen to the next level?

If yes, search for an investment class or an investment club. Write down the name of 5 options you could engage in within the next 60 days to be intentional about becoming move savvy about investing.

If you are not yet investing

6. What has been the #1 fear keeping you from investing?

7. How can you overcome that fear?

8. When do you believe you could start investing?

9. What are 3 action steps you could take in the next 30 days to reach that goal?

10. If you don't have the means to invest right now, the next best thing you can do is learn all that you can, so when you are ready, you will be equipped to do so successfully. What will be the first podcast you listen to, YouTube video you will watch, or book you will read (after you finish this one) to help you get started on your investment learning journey?

For everyone

11. If your financial situation allowed for it, what is one emerging industry or technology you would regularly invest in?

12. If you are employed, does your benefits program offer any complimentary sessions with a financial advisor?

If so, set up an appointment to review your investment portfolio, your allocation distributions, and the funds offered by your employer. Take advantage of all free resources.

13. Generational wealth and generational knowledge go hand-in-hand. Will you commit to creating wealth for future generations and sharing the knowledge you learned to help create that wealth?

If yes, write down the name of at least one person younger than you, whether it be your child(ren), another family member, or someone you mentor and commit to regularly sharing the financial investment knowledge you gain on your own learning journey.

CHAPTER EIGHTEEN

Your Habits
Drafting Your Blueprint

> *"I don't think it is an exaggeration to say that financial literacy, economic empowerment, and wealth-building is going to be the last leg of the civil rights movement. Because one step toward financial literacy takes you two steps toward personal empowerment."*
>
> – Russell Simmons, Serial Entrepreneurs

It will take both macro shifts and micro changes to knock out the wealth gap and bolster our average net worth as black Americans. The change starts with us and our commitment to personal empowerment. We must be thoughtful with every dollar that enters our checking and savings accounts. We need to daily execute our plans for how we leverage, distribute, and invest our funds. It is up to us to become educated, set healthy boundaries, and progress over time towards building a sustainable financial legacy. With a mindset steeped in an abundant view of resources and solid financial tools and knowledge in our hands, we can reach the goal of attaining a #7-Figure Net Worth and beyond much more of the norm within our community.

Writing Your Own Story Ending

In our story, while Shonna excelled in reaching her goals—she had her challenges as well, but her Grandpa was a grounding influence in her life. Without his wisdom, she could have easily succumbed to poor financial decisions and habits. What made Shonna different? She refused to surrender, and she fought for her goals. You can too! In looking back at Shonna's story, there were a few key things that she did really well, including:

1. Holding firm on her position that using credit cards were a no-no—starting with refusing sign-up offers in college.

2. Resisting the lure to show and tell regarding her income and wealth. As an example, she maintained her used car as long as possible.

3. Overcoming the temptation to increase her spending proportionate to her salary increases. This one was very hard, as Shonna had to forgo many things she could have easily 'afforded' with her salary.

As you can see, Shonna made better financial choices earlier, which changed the trajectory of her net worth. Not because her life was carefree, but instead she actively invested in raising her financial knowledge with her income. Every time Shonna gained finances, she followed the proverb and applied truth, wisdom, and understanding (Proverbs 23:23). She acted on what she learned. For Shonna, her financial future was always hers to direct.

With Shonna's positive influence and presence as an accountability partner combined with his updated habits, Shawn was making positive strides as well. At the last meeting with his financial coach, he finalized his plan to gain a #7-Figure Net Worth. While it would take several years, he could breathe easy knowing he had a solid plan in place.

Shawn also gained more confidence in talking about finances. During a conversation at a cookout, Shawn was surprised to learn that his high school classmate and friend Samuel had been making positive money moves. He had already accumulated a positive net worth of almost $200,000 towards his goal of becoming a millionaire.

Looking at the way Samuel lived his life working at a garage and driving an old car, Shawn would have never guessed. Samuel shared that his uncle had always put him on game since he was young and gave him books about finances when he was a teenager. He made a decision in high school to learn a trade instead of going the student loan financed college route.

Samuel confided that he actually owned the garage most people thought he just worked at. After working at a shop for a few years, one of the two owners decided to retire. With the money Samuel saved from his frugal lifestyle and a personal loan from his uncle, he bought out that owner's share of the company. He didn't advertise that fact, though. Shawn was super impressed and gave him the card of his financial coach and told Samuel to reach out if he wanted to fine-tune his plan. Samuel said he definitely would.

The conversations about finances continued to pop-up. During a double-date dinner that Shawn and Shonna attended together, he also learned more personal financial details from his boy Julian and his wife, Danielle. They confided that after really focusing on reducing their spending and making lifestyle changes, they were now only $1,000 away from gaining a positive net worth.

Julian shared some of the challenges they faced early on in their financial journey together. Smiling, Danielle chimed in that she was proud of their growth as a couple. She excitedly shared that they would begin to work toward a million-dollar net worth mark next month with guidance from their financial coach. With a grin on his face, Julian shared how he was also adding an additional income stream using his love of drones to take pictures for real estate listings. He was even going to get a tax right off for buying his "toys" now!

Assembling His Crew

Excited about his newfound knowledge and wanting to keep the dialogue and education going, Shawn asked the four of them—Shonna, Samuel, Julian, and Danielle—to meet for a monthly dinner party. It would be a potluck (*he was learning*). The dinners would also provide a safe space to discuss their path, progress, challenges, and opportunities towards obtaining their respective #7-Figure Net Worth goals. They all enthusiastically agreed.

He asked for them to be transparent. He requested that they each share their current personal balance sheets. He also asked for their future one, that they completed with their financial coach. The future balance sheet illustrated what their financial portfolio will look like after reaching their million-dollar net worth goal. With his coach's permission, he shared the template with Shonna for her to fill out. After a little nudging about pushing past the discomfort, a few words of trash talk about being scary to his boys, and reminders about confidentiality, they *finally* all sent them over.

As we close out this section on habits, let's review their current and planned future balance sheets as inspiration for what we can achieve in our own lives.

Shawn Before
Personal Balance Sheet

Protection

Will / Trust	Liability Insurance		Life Insurance	Disability Insurance
No	$ 300,000.00		$ 145,000.00	60% of Salary

Assets			Liabilities	
Cash Savings	$ 500.00		Personal Loan	-
Stocks/Bonds/ETFs	$ 4,986.00		Student Loan	$ 17,000.00
IRA	-		Mortgage	-
401k	$ 15,847.00		Car Loan	$ 34,407.00
Annuity	-		Business Loan	-
Business Income	-		Credit Card Debt	$ 12,345.00
Cash Value Ins	-		**Total Liabilities**	**$ 63,752.00**
Real Estate	-			
Total Assets	**$ 21,333.00**			

Cash Flow

Gross Salary	$ 145,000.00		Total Monthly Income	$ 4.350.00
Other Income	-		Total Monthly Expenses	$ 3,750.00
			Net Monthly Cash Flow	$ 600.00

Total Net Worth

-$42,419

Shawn After 19 Years
Personal Balance Sheet

Protection

Will / Trust	Liability Insurance		Life Insurance	Disability Insurance
Yes Will	$ 1,000,000.00		$ 1,500,000,00	70% of Salary

Assets			Liabilities	
Cash Savings	$ 26,100.00		Personal Loan	-
Stocks/Bonds/ETFs	$ 35,846.00		Student Loan	-
IRA (Roth)	$ 105,898.00		Mortgage	$ 200,000.00
401k	$ 226,987.00		Car Loan	-
Annuity	$ 200,456.00		Business Loan	-
Business Income	-		Credit Card Debt	-
Cash Value Ins	$ 105,697.00		**Total Liabilities**	**$ 200,000.00**
Real Estate	$ 507,064.00			
Total Assets	**$ 1,208,048.00**			

Cash Flow

Gross Salary	$ 175,000.00		Total Monthly Income	$ 5,115.00
Other Income	-		Total Monthly Expenses	$ 3,750.00
			Net Monthly Cash Flow	$ 1,365.00

Total Net Worth

$ 1,008,048.00

Shonna Before
Personal Balance Sheet

Protection

Will / Trust	Liability Insurance	Life Insurance	Disability Insurance
No	$ 100,000.00	$ 90,000.00	50% of Salary

Assets		Liabilities	
Cash Savings	$ 9,000.00	Personal Loan	-
Stocks/Bonds/ETFs	-	Student Loan	$ 12,000.00
IRA (Roth)	-	Mortgage	$ 225,000.00
401k	$ 42,000.00	Car Loan	-
Annuity	-	Business Loan	-
Business Income	-	Credit Card Debt	-
Cash Value Ins	-	**Total Liabilities**	**$ 237,000.00**
Real Estate	$ 330,000.00		
Total Assets	**$ 381,000.00**		

Cash Flow

Gross Salary	$ 90,000.00	Total Monthly Income	$ 5,400.00
Other Income	-	Total Monthly Expenses	$ 2,255.00
		Net Monthly Cash Flow	$ 3,145.00

Total Net Worth

$ 144,000.00

Shonna After 12 Years
Personal Balance Sheet

Protection

Will / Trust	Liability Insurance	Life Insurance	Disability Insurance
Trust	$ 1,000,000.00	$ 600,000,00	70% of Salary

Assets		Liabilities	
Cash Savings	$ 95,000.00	Personal Loan	-
Stocks/Bonds/ETFs	$ 75,000.00	Student Loan	-
IRA (Roth)	$ 30,000.00	Mortgage	$ 20,000.00
401k	$ 500,000.00	Car Loan	-
Annuity	-	Business Loan	-
Business Income	-	Credit Card Debt	-
Cash Value Ins	$ 120,000.00	**Total Liabilities**	**$ 20,000.00**
Real Estate	$ 420,000.00		
Total Assets	**$ 1,070,000.00**		

Cash Flow

Gross Salary	$ 115,000.00	Total Monthly Income	$ 9,583.33
Other Income	-	Total Monthly Expenses	$ 3,450.00
		Net Monthly Cash Flow	$ 6,133.33

Total Net Worth

$ 1,050,000.00

Danielle & Julian Before
Personal Balance Sheet

Protection

Will / Trust	Liability Insurance	Life Insurance	Disability Insurance
Will	$ 300,000.00	$ 700,000.00	50% of Salary

Assets		Liabilities	
Cash Savings	$ 10,000.00	Personal Loan	-
Stocks/Bonds/ETFs	$ 5,000.00	Student Loan	$ 100,000.00
IRA (Roth)	-	Mortgage	$ 345,000.00
401k	$ 75,000.00	Car Loan	$ 20,000.00
Annuity	-	Business Loan	-
Business Income	-	Credit Card Debt	$ 26,000.00
Cash Value Ins	-	**Total Liabilities**	**$ 491,000.00**
Real Estate	$ 400,000.00		
Total Assets	**$ 490,000.00**		

Cash Flow

Gross Salary	$ 190,000.00	Total Monthly Income	$ 12,350.00
Other Income	-	Total Monthly Expenses	$ 9,849.00
		Net Monthly Cash Flow	$ 2,501.00

Total Net Worth

-$1,000

Danielle & Julian After 17 Years
Personal Balance Sheet

Protection

Will / Trust	Liability Insurance	Life Insurance	Disability Insurance
Will and Trust	$ 2,000,000.00	$ 2,500,000,00	75% of Salary

Assets		Liabilities	
Cash Savings	$ 60,000.00	Personal Loan	-
Stocks/Bonds/ETFs	$ 305,000.00	Student Loan	-
IRA (Roth)	$ 100,000.00	Mortgage	$ 500,000.00
401k	$ 203,000.00	Car Loan	-
Annuity	-	Business Loan	-
Business Ownership	$ 40,000.00	Credit Card Debt	$ 1,000.00
Cash Value Ins	$ 230,000.00	**Total Liabilities**	**$ 501,000.00**
Real Estate	$ 700,000.00		
Total Assets	**$ 1,638,000.00**		

Cash Flow

Gross Salary	$ 225,000.00	Total Monthly Income	$ 22,083.33
Other Income	$ 40,000.00	Total Monthly Expenses	$ 8,200.00
		Net Monthly Cash Flow	$ 13,883.33

Total Net Worth

$ 1,137,000.00

Samuel Before
Personal Balance Sheet

Protection

Will / Trust	Liability Insurance		Life Insurance	Disability Insurance
No	$ 300,000.00		$ 5,000.00	-

Assets			Liabilities	
Cash Savings	$ 55,000.00		Personal Loan	$ 40,000.00
Stocks/Bonds/ETFs	-		Student Loan	-
IRA (Roth)	-		Mortgage	$ 80,000.00
401k	-		Car Loan	-
Annuity	-		Business Loan	-
Business Income	$ 160,000.00		Credit Card Debt	-
Cash Value Ins	-		**Total Liabilities**	**$ 120,000.00**
Real Estate	$ 100,000.00			
Total Assets	**$ 315,000.00**			

Cash Flow

Gross Salary	-		Total Monthly Income	$ 5,200.00
Other Income	$ 80,000.00		Total Monthly Expenses	$ 1,900.00
			Net Monthly Cash Flow	$ 3,300.00

Total Net Worth

$ 195,000.00

Samuel After 18 Years
Personal Balance Sheet

Protection

Will / Trust	Liability Insurance	Key Person Insurance	Life Insurance	Disability Insurance
No	$ 300,000.00	$ 250,000.00	$ 500,000,00	75% of Salary

Assets		Liabilities	
Cash Savings	$ 145,000.00	Personal Loan	-
Stocks/Bonds/ETFs	$ 195,000.00	Student Loan	-
IRA (Roth)	$ 255,000.00	Mortgage	$ 45,000.00
401k	-	Car Loan	-
Annuity	$ 35,000.00	Business Loan	-
Business Ownership	$ 125,000.00	Credit Card Debt	-
Cash Value Ins	-	**Total Liabilities**	**$ 45,000.00**
Real Estate	$ 300,000.00		
Total Assets	**$ 1,055,000.00**		

Cash Flow

Gross Salary	-	Total Monthly Income	$ 8,125.00
Other Income	$ 125,000.00	Total Monthly Expenses	$ 2,700.00
		Net Monthly Cash Flow	$ 5,425.00

Total Net Worth

$ 1,010,000.00

Your Habits
Drafting Your Blueprint

Now it's your turn! As we come to a close on the habits part of your journey, let's create an outline for your own personal financial blueprint and walk towards high net worth and to create intergenerational wealth. I know that some of these questions you may have answered in previous worksheets. When you are building a new muscle, there is power in repetition, and I also want you to see all of the key components in one place. While I highly recommend that you work with a financial coach and a financial advisor to fine-tune your own plan. Hopefully, this will get you started.

#7-Figure Net Worth Blueprint Starter

1. Who will be your accountability partners in your progress towards this goal?

2. In pursuit of a #7-Figure Net Worth, are there 1-3 people you can create a monthly dialogue with, share this book's concepts, and create accountability? If so, reach out, get a commitment from these individuals, and schedule your monthly meets, whether in person or virtual.

3. Depreciating assets are more of an expense and less of an investment. What are 3 depreciating assets you can reduce your recurring spend on?

4. What 3 appreciating assets do you want to focus on investing in? By what date do you want to start this acquisition process? Add the value you would like to have for each asset category one year from now.

5. Who are the experts you need to talk to gain more knowledge about investing in each of these types of appreciating assets? Over the next month, reach out and schedule a time to speak with each of them. Space out your sessions so you have time to reflect on knowledge acquired from each session.

6. How much do you want to have saved one year from now? Moving forward, what percentage of your income will you save monthly?

7. What causes are you passionate about that you want to give impactfully to? What amount do you desire to contribute to each cause over the next year?

8. What are 3 actions you can take within the next 30 days to increase your primary active income source? Who will be your accountability partner you will share it with? *Note: If you may not have that person currently in your circle, the members of our Facebook group are always here to celebrate with you.*

9. What additional income stream(s) do you want to add? Are at least one of these streams passive? How much income do you want additional streams to bring in over the next year?

10. Choose one of the income streams from question 7. What are 3 actions you can take in the next 30 days to get this income stream started?

11. What 3 strategies will you use to reduce your debt (if applicable)? How quickly can you begin to implement these strategies?

12. What 3 steps will you take to increase your credit score (if applicable)? By when will you complete each action?

13. What is the name and contact information of three insurance agents or brokers you will discuss your current or potential insurance products with? Write down the date and time you will do a consultation to understand their fee structure and decide if they are the right fit for you.

14. What adjustments do you need to make with a) the type of insurance you cur-rently have or b) the amount of coverage you have, or both?

15. What negative mindset(s) will you be most diligent about no longer allowing to influence your financial decisions?

16. What new mindset(s) are you replacing it with? What method are you using to ensure you hear, see, and implement that new mindset daily?

17. What aspect of relationships involving money will you adjust in pursuit of your financial goals? Why is it important to you that these relationships change?

18. What day will you have conversations with each of those people? Who will be your accountability partner you will share the outcome of these conversations with?

19. What are the names and contact information of three financial coaches you could work with towards your goals? Write down the date and time you will consult with each coach to understand their fee structure and decide if they are the right fit for you.

20. What are the names and contact information of three investment advisors you could work with towards your goals? Write down the date and time you will consult to understand their fee structure and decide if they are the right fit for you. Don't forget to check if these consults may be offered free through your employer (if applicable).

21. What is your current net worth?

22. What net worth goals will you work towards achieving over the next:

    a. 12 months?

    b. 3 years?

    c. 5 years?

    d. 10 years?

    e. 20 years?

23. What is your desired asset distribution to make up each of these goals? You can use the above scenarios as an example if you would like.

24. Thinking about the progress you will make over the next year, what is one way you will celebrate a year from now when you reach these goals?

While there are multiple facets to becoming an HNWI, you can absolutely achieve these goals with determination and discipline! Now, let's talk about the one thing that could undermine your ability to make meaningful progress if we don't address it: your mindset!

CHAPTER NINETEEN

Your Mindset
Inherited Money Mindsets

"Not everything that is faced can be changed,

but nothing can be changed until it is faced."

– James Baldwin

Understanding your numbers and establishing sound fiscal habits are essential. However, without having a healthy mindset in place, you will find your journey to achieve a #7-Figure Net Worth to be much more difficult or undermined completely.

We have to get our minds right!

Look, we all know it and feel it—the struggle out here to obtain wealth is real! As black Americans, many factors press against our minds and impede our progress towards gaining and maintaining intergenerational wealth.

As we've discussed, one of the primary external factors is that we have fewer dollars to work with since systematic racism is messing with our paychecks. Literally, black Americans, on average, have lower median wages than our white counterparts.

We dived into how our financial progress is also challenged in one of the main ways of creating wealth – homeownership. Given the challenges of systematic racism in banking and lending, we literally pay more interest on average for every dollar we borrow. That has a tremendous increase in many of our 10-, 15-, or 30-year mortgages' total cost.

If that weren't enough, we reviewed how structural discrimination has resulted in home appraisals in predominantly African American neighborhoods receive lower valuations. Even when we have homes of similar aesthetics, construction quality, and square footage in other areas!

Although, I have been pointing out external factors (and probably could add 50–11 more). I'm definitely not here to harp on "the problem" or "the man." As my line sister asked, "Is this is about education or excuses?" This is about education. **We can indeed move forward despite these challenges. We just have to remain aware that these external factors will try to trip us up in our individual journeys to wealth.**

Now that we have talked through the various external factors, it is now of equal or greater importance to look at the *internal factors* that also impede our wealth building – including our personal and cultural mindsets. **Many mindsets can impact one's wealth journey.** However, in this #7–Figure Net Worth paradigm, we will focus on five concepts in our culture that may permeate our mentality about money.

As we move together towards meaningfully stacking our bills, some of the mindset challenges may include:

1. Focusing on taking care of the generation before us instead of creating a financial legacy for generations that follow us.

2. Leveraging insurance only as a defensive strategy and not deploying specific insurance products offensively as tools to create wealth.

3. Buying an abundance of depreciating assets that deflate our financial portfolios versus intentionally gaining appreciating assets.

4. Working hard only in our active income streams rather than diversify our efforts to also create passive income streams.

5. Giving when guilted and saving sporadically instead of giving impactfully, saving intentionally, and investing strategically.

Let's unpack the impact of some of these inherited money mindsets with this next worksheet.

Your Mindset

Inherited Money Mindsets

1. Between internal and external factors, which do you believe play the most prominent role in holding black Americans back from attaining wealth?

2. Have any of these five (5) mindsets impacted you thus far? If so, how?

3. Which of these mindsets would you identify as being hardest for you to shift?

4. Have you seen any of these mindsets impact the financial journeys of your friends or family members? If so, how?

5. Are there other mindsets, whether positively or negatively, within our culture that you feel have shaped you personally or impacted overall attitudes toward wealth?

6. Do you believe there is a way to impact future generations' financial legacy while still supporting the generations before you? If so, how can you achieve this?

7. According to your answer to question 2, how can you challenge and eliminate your mindset challenge(s)?

8. Hoping the next generation will be better than we are, how can you influence our community's culture to move away from these inherited mindsets?

Find us on Facebook

We want to hear from you! Post other mindsets that you think have impacted our journey towards financial success and inter-generational wealth in our #7-Figure Net Worth Facebook group.

CHAPTER TWENTY

Your Mindset
Extended Family Impact

> *"Being responsible sometimes means pissing people off."*
>
> – Collin Powell

Back in the '90s, Kris Kross made it popular to wear our clothes backward (yes, I'm aging myself—but the millennials reading this remember, right?). "Kris Kross'll make ya (jump jump)." Yes, it was the trend and very fashionable to literally put your clothes on the wrong way. Nowadays, you won't catch anyone wearing their clothes that way. Yet there are other ways we find ourselves as a culture living a bit backward.

Fast forward to today, and you, like me, may be wondering about modern Black America, *Where are our wealth gains?* Despite our numerous strides in Black America in education, business, and financial increase over the years, the wealth gap between black and white Americans is continually increasing. The question then becomes, why?

According to the Institute on Assets and Social Policy, who conducted a 25-year study, "white Americans are five times more likely to inherit than black Americans (36 percent to 7 percent, respectively)." While both whites and blacks may receive an inheritance, white Americans tend to receive nearly five times more. What's up with that?

Our cultural norms impact how we perceive, plan, and feel about inheritances. One factor may be related to the reversal of an adult child's responsibilities. Whereas other cultures focus on leaving an inheritance to their children, we place pressure on *our* kids to "make it." So that when we become adults, we can take care of our parents and extended family members. This mindset significantly impacts wealth accumulation to the point that some experts have coined this phenomenon as the "black tax."

The "black tax" is defined as income that black professionals regularly give to their families to support them. The term "family" is parallel to anyone connected to us—because it could be a brother, a sister, a play-cousin, and very often parents. Somewhere along the line, black middle and upper-class professionals have felt an immense responsibility to offer financial resources in some form to those around us. Often, such support takes the form of monetary gifts to family members who are "struggling."

Wrestling with internal pressure and external expectations, "successful black professionals" have the consistent pressure and expectations to "show love" to those around us. There is absolutely nothing wrong with providing financial help to those we care about. However, it can at points cross the line of stunting our ability to accumulate and creating lasting wealth. If we pour out money *without limitation*, there will be very little left for saving and investing in our future—which includes our children. No matter the amount of internal struggle and shade we may receive at first, we must find a healthy balance. The financial destiny of our children and grandchildren depends upon it.

It is not even just a budgeting issue for most modern black Americans. It is also a deeply rooted emotional one. Thomas K.R. Stovall, the founder of WeUnifyTech, explains, "***I didn't always know how to say no***, and for years I would put myself in peril, trying to help other people. I think it is imperative for folks who find themselves in this situation to learn how to say no, without guilt." For us, who follow Christ's teachings, saying, "Yes" and "No," is not only important—it is biblical (Matthew 5:37).

Many of us have become a consistent source of financial support for our family members—which some of us are happy to do. Yet, some may do it grudgingly and out of guilt. As real as the guilt trips can be, I definitely don't advocate for the latter. When we do give, we should do so joyfully. The Bible provides us with this instruction. "Every man according as he purposeth in his heart, so let him give; not grudgingly, or of necessity: for God loveth a cheerful giver" (II Corinthians 9:7 King James Version).

Do you sometimes feel resentful of those that you are giving to? If so, you may want to take an extra step of journaling or talking to a counselor about those feelings. Our emotional and mental health related to finances is a critical and valued part of our wealth equation.

Excavating to find out the root cause of those emotions is equally important work to do on your financial journey. It may be uncomfortable or even, in some cases, painful. Still, it is important to not separate the numbers on our spreadsheets from the sentiment in our souls that drive the behavior generating those numbers:

1. Do that work to get to the root.

2. Identify any changes you need to make within your mindset about giving to extended family or adjustments.

3. Communicate any changes you need to make in those relationships to move to a healthier place.

Get clear in your heart and mind about helping your loved ones financially. You can then allocate a specific line item each month in your budget to support extended family and friends if you can afford it. Once those funds are depleted within a month, if something comes up, we simply say, "We don't have it!"

For my husband and I (and more so *me* due to emotional connections), it was tough saying no at first. Sometimes we only offered a fraction of what was requested because that was all we had left in that budget category for that month. At times, we have even had to ignore the 'side-eye' that others gave us based on their perception of our resources. Yet, we know the legacy that we want to leave – so our decisions empower us to challenge the expectation others may try to project upon us of giving without limits.

If we are intentional, many of us can find ourselves in the best position to both help others *and* create sustainable wealth. Our opportunity is to provide financial family support with boundaries while also creating heirlooms of generational wealth.

Here is a practical example of boundaries. After noticing a pattern of repetitive requests without any circumstantial progress, a friend of mine will say "Yes," one more time but also hand out a book about budgeting or financial principles with the funds they ask for. She makes it a requirement that they have to have completed reading the book before they ask again. So perhaps that may be something you can adopt. Before you position yourself for that final "No," you may consider gifting that loved one with this book or another. You can choose to provide them wisdom along with financial resources to support them in their journey.

Wherever you decide to draw your line, you may find it emotionally challenging at first (like I did). You may find that protecting your immediate four walls and descendants is of top priority, so you don't struggle with it (like my husband). Either way, you may find that as you stay consistent in your posture, many begin to respect your boundaries, drive, and goals. Say "No," to requests that don't align with your personal financial viewpoints or that will result in unwise financial decisions. Think of all the inter-generational wealth you can create with those funds. Envision the melanin "trust fund" babies that can be a part of your financial heritage.

Some of your children and great-grandchildren may use their inherited wealth to jumpstart their education, to start world-changing businesses, or to realize their homeownership dreams. You must think about those coming behind you. As wise wealth managers, we must grow our capital through our influence.

What we hold in our hands now—impact what our children will hold. Your children's hands are the future family hands of stewardship. Imagine what would happen if you were the last person in your family unable to do what you need or even what you want because of a lack of financial resources. Now let's imagine together a future that is generationally wealthier with this next worksheet.

Your Mindset

Extended Family Impact

1. Think: What messages about finances or financial responsibilities have I internalized from the following people?

   i. Parents?

   ii. Extended Family?

   iii. Friends?

   iv. Community?

2. Do you currently provide financial support to anyone consistently? Who receives your support, and why? Has your financial support truly helped them move forward in life, or is it enabling them to maintain their current habits?

3. If you remove emotions from the equation, would you still provide financial support? Why or why not?

4. What, if any adjustments do you need to make to the financial support you provide?

5. What, if any, boundaries do you need to set as you become an effective financial resource for friends and family?

6. Are you concerned that these boundaries could hurt your relationships with family and friends? If so, how would you lovingly explain why these boundaries are positive for everyone?

7. Describe in detail the dream financial reality you want your grandchildren, god-children, nieces, nephews, or those you create a legacy for via charity to grow up with. What successes would they be able to achieve? What type of mind-set would they live with? What barriers would they be able to eliminate? What amazing future would they be able to create for the generation after them?

This may be difficult for many, but practice lovingly saying "No." As you move towards shifting your mindset and creating boundaries, one of the hardest parts will be resisting the urge to get back to your old habits of supporting without boundaries. Create this new habit now by getting comfortable saying "No," while at the same time offering to use your knowledge to help them get on the same path as you. You are still supporting them, just in a new way, which will educate and empower them to get on the journey to their own financial independence.

8. Suppose you adopt the approach of budgeting your financial support for extended family and friends. What monthly budgeted amount will allow you to take care of your expenses and meet your savings and investing goals?

CHAPTER TWENTY-ONE

Your Mindset
Letter to Money

> *"Financial health is having a conscious and purposeful relationship with money."*
>
> *– Brad Klontz, Financial Psychologist*

For any relationship with an "It's Complicated" status, one of the best ways to achieve happiness and health may be through complete honesty and laying all of your cards on the table. In this worksheet, that is exactly what I want you to do by addressing your current relationship with money. I want you to really shatter those walls that surround your current money mindsets.

I want you to break open your defining money experiences and examine them. I want you to observe how you feel or what you think when specific finance-related encounters take place. Whether abundance or lack, positive or negative, empowering or traumatizing, examine your thoughts and feelings related to money.

In that space, I want you to write it all down. You can use the space below, open up a document on your computer, find a separate journal, or pop open an audio app to speak it out on your phone. I want you to write or speak a letter to money. Don't worry if it isn't perfect—no such thing here. The goal is to write your raw and authentic sentiment about money at this very moment.

Here's an example that may be helpful.

Dear Money,

I feel conflicted and incompetent in dealing with you. I watched my parents struggle to get you. I watched my Grandmother stuff dollars in cans for years and still leave this world without enough of you. I watched my cousin die in the street because of you. And I heard people in my church say that "Money is evil." It's just been way too much. As a child always hearing that, I secretly thought at first, it was a sin to have you. Then I realized that clearly, these folks weren't doing a good job reading what's in the black and the white. I finally read the Bible for myself, and there were the words "Love of Money was Evil" just as clear as day. I was grateful and thought to myself as an adult, "That's a relief. I can now match up to my faith with my ambition and hustle."

However, that bit of clarity didn't stop all of my confusion. I've continued to run into one problem after another dealing with you. People repeatedly told me that if I didn't love money—then I shouldn't obsess over it. It's kind of hard to do that when you have never had enough—now or while growing up. Now that I see more and more of you, I'm starting to feel burned out constantly because of you. I work tirelessly week in and week out just to stack you. Then as soon as you arrived, I received constant requests from family and friends to have most of you. If this is supposed to be the "come up," why does it feel like I am only treading water with you. Like a hamster on a wheel, I feel like I'm getting nowhere with you.

Finally, fed up! I asked God, "Why in the world would I listen to Him if I am constantly struggling!" I'm bringing you in, but you seem to leave as soon as you come. I pay all my bills but after that that you're gone. God is patient with me, and I imagine He laughed. He led me to His word and showed me He said more about you than I ever knew. He led me to read Matthew 25:14–26 and Luke 19:11–26. From these scriptures, I started to learn more about managing you.

I learned that I was your steward, and with wisdom, He would show me what to do. I've read Proverbs 10:4 and Proverbs 10:22 every day until I had finally got it in my head that you were a tool. At last, I finally stopped blaming God because I lacked you! Instead, I worked from His guidance on how best to manage you. I was skeptical at first, but as my wisdom grew, so did your presence in my savings and investments. More importantly, I studied II Corinthians 9:6–10 and learned when to give you on purpose, not just when requested.

Now, our relationship is good and still getting better. I still have some places to heal, and the scars still have their presence. Yet, I'm learning that my heritage is to be royal with you and not just a peasant. Now my relationship has improved with you—money! I will never go back to the life I had before. I'm figuring you out money, and you'll continue to stay around way longer than ever before. We are in this for life and hopefully until the next. I expect you to do great things one day—especially with my kids. So know that I wrote this because I wanted my feelings to be true—money we started off rough, but I'm going to finish with you.

Blessings,

Deante Richards-Smith*

———

Note: Deante Richards-Smith is a **fictional** name.

Now it is your turn!

Write your letter to money in a way that is "No Holds Barred!" No worries if the letter shows the conflicts you've felt. The goal is to examine how you can change your relationship with money. **One more thing**: *Once you have written this letter, save a copy somewhere you can retrieve the letter. Set a calendar date 90 days from now and finish this book.* After 90 days or when you finish the book (whichever is first), write another letter to money. **Compare the two letters (before and after). See how your relationship with money has changed since finishing the book and all of the worksheets!** This may be a great way to document the evolution of your financial mindsets from year to year.

Your Mindset
Letter to Money

· ·

Dear Money,

Sincerely,

CHAPTER TWENTY-TWO

Your Mindset

Renewing Your Mind

The Role of Financial Affirmations

> *Stop imitating the ideals and opinions of the culture around you,*
>
> *but be inwardly transformed by the Holy Spirit through a total reformation of how you think.*
>
> *This will empower you to discern God's will as you live a beautiful life,*
>
> *satisfying and perfect in his eyes.*
>
> *– Romans 12:2 (Passion Translation)*

For me facing my relationship with money was a surprisingly emotional experience.

It took many hours of reading, studying, prayer, and reflection to come to a place where I could genuinely reprogram my thoughts, fears, and insecurities related to money.

One mindset I really struggled with was the notion, "I am not good with money."

I thought this was true because I grew up in poverty, and no one ever taught me about money management and stewardship. The fact that I believed my ineptitude regarding finances to be true for so long is likely the biggest irony of *me* doing this #7-Figure Net Worth project.

For years, that wrong belief fought against me. Even though I gained insight into money in my own life—working hard to move past my circumstance, those emotions kept me from feeling like I could share all of the knowledge I had diligently acquired.

Not until I did the uncomfortable work and finally faced the fear head-on—that mindset, that lie—was I finally released. Released to shape my mind to include placing a value on the knowledge I have accumulated and a passion for the financial well-being of upcoming black American generations.

Released to deepen my knowledge base of appreciating assets and insurance.

Free to be creative in passive and active income streams.

Released to save intentionally and really give impactfully.

Acting on these ideas brought the kind of freedom I offer you now today. Yet it started with challenging my mindsets, facing my fears, and confronting them with knowledge + action for the life we now live.

So, what's your story?

How can you face the lies that you believe about money?

What could you change if you overcome messages you always heard growing up and never took the time to scrutinize or challenge?

What could you change if you examine the messages you've always heard and kept only the good?

How will you overcome any harmful ideas you have internalized and replace them with ideas for a better future?

The time to figure out this process is now! It's time to renew your mind and expose the thinking that may be holding you back! You can grow! Believe in your impact! Move towards your craziest and scariest financial dreams! You can get there. Let's first disconnect, though, from the baggage that may be holding you back and making your journey way harder than it needs to be. In this next worksheet, I want you to identify those ratty mindsets that are limiting you and identify new mantras and ways of thinking to replace the stagnant ones.

Positive Financial Affirmations

I am committed! I will increase the wealth on my personal balance sheet to build a better future for my children.

I can achieve a seven-figure net worth! I am empowered to increase my personal net worth to a million dollars and more.

I'm creating generational wealth! Because of my actions today, my children will inherit generational wealth.

I highly value appreciating assets. I will spend more money on appreciating assets and less on depreciating ones.

I have financial discipline. I will budget and reconcile monthly.

I am financially literate and educated about investing. I will continually learn more about investment options.

I will hustle, man! I will actively find ways to make passive income.

I can practice self-denial. I will no longer purchase things on impulse.

I take ownership of my financial situation! I am responsible for building a better financial life for myself.

I can have great credit! I will make sure my bill payments are made on time.

I have self-restraint! I will not touch any money in my savings account for personal recreational use.

I walk in financial wisdom. My net worth will increase because of the wise financial decisions I made today.

Scriptural Financial Affirmations (NKJV)

I am favor! Psalm 5:12 For You, O Lord, will bless the righteous; With favor You will surround him as with a shield.

I have wisdom. God gives me understanding! Proverbs 4:7 Wisdom is the principal thing; Therefore get wisdom. And in all your getting, get understanding.

I hear God's voice, and I am elevated! Deuteronomy 28:1-2 Blessings on Obedience: 1 Now it shall come to pass, if you diligently obey the voice of the Lord your God, to observe carefully all His commandments which I command you today, that the Lord your God will set you high above all nations of the earth. 2 And all these blessings shall come upon you and overtake you, because you obey the voice of the Lord your God.

I believe God can do anything in finances! Ephesians 3:20 Now to Him who is able to do exceedingly abundantly above all that we ask or think, according to the power that works in us.

I have wealth and good health to enjoy it! 3 John 2 Beloved, I pray that you may prosper in all things and be in health, just as your soul prospers.

I make my way prosperous! I have good success! Joshua 1:8 This Book of the Law shall not depart from your mouth, but you(a) shall meditate in it day and night, that you may observe to do according to all that is written in it. For then you will make your way prosperous, and then you will have good success.

I honor God and respect what he says. Because I follow His principles, wealth and riches are in my house! Psalm 112:1-3 Praise the Lord! Blessed is the man who fears the Lord, Who delights greatly in His commandments. His descendants will be mighty on earth; The generation of the upright will be blessed. Wealth and riches will be in his house, And his righteousness endures forever.

I believe in wealth being in my life! II Corinthians 8:9 For you know the grace of our Lord Jesus Christ, that though He was rich, yet for your sakes He became poor, that you through His poverty might become rich.

I am diligent—that brings wealth in my life! Proverbs 10:4 He who has a slack hand becomes poor, But the hand of the diligent makes rich.

I am blessed—that means wealth comes without sorrow! Proverbs 10:22 The blessing of the Lord makes one rich, And He adds no sorrow with it.

Your Mindset

Renewing Your Mind

1. Before reading this book, did you have any secret or maybe not so secret insecurities related to finances? What are they? Using affirmations, do you believe that you can begin to rid yourself of these thoughts and emotions?

2. If you are able to release yourself from these insecurities, what new emotions do you hope to feel?

3. Revisit the list of scriptural affirmations. Which one gives you the most confidence and inspiration? Choose one and make an effort to speak it out loud three times a day. When you wake up, at noon, and before you lay your head down at night. After doing it every day for a week, write down how it made you feel? Did it brighten your day? Give you more confidence? Inspire you to keep going through a hard time? Write it down.

4. How will you reinforce these positive financial mindsets daily (sticky notes, phone apps, etc.)?

5. Share your preferred method and include two or three of the new financial affir-mations you have chosen to speak or listen to daily.

6. Going back to Romans 12:2 and being honest with yourself, do you feel you have been too influenced by the ideas and opinions of those around you? If so, how can you begin to make room to include the Holy Spirit in your daily life to help you start your personal transformation to a peaceful and satisfying life?

7. After learning these affirmation practices, what family member or friend can benefit from a renewed mindset? Choose someone and for the next five days, send them a new affirmation every day. Come back after a week and write down their response and how it made you feel to bring positivity into someone else's life.

Multiple books speak to this topic. Here are a couple of the ones that I have found helpful along my journey!

Battlefield of the Mind
Joyce Meyer

———

Heal Your Relationship with Money
Kara Stevens

———

The Soul of Money
Lynne Twist

———

Scripture Confessions for Finances:
Life-Changing Words of Faith for Every Day
Keith Provance

Find us on Facebook

Choose a method that will help you to daily bring positive financial affirmations into your life. You may opt for the "Being Mary Jane" method where Mary Jane, a prominent television anchor (played by Gabrielle Union), posted sticky notes all over her house, including her sliding glass doors and mirrors affirmations and goals. You may prefer an electronic approach using an affirmation app or creating your own reminders in the calendar on your phone. Choose whatever method you find most comfortable, and you can build daily consistency with.

Which method will you choose to reinforce these positive financial mindsets daily?

Share your preferred method in our #7-Figure Net Worth Facebook Group and include two or three of the new financial affirmations you have chosen to speak or listen to daily.

You may never know how one of your chosen affirmations may help someone to renew their mind as well!

Money and Mental Health

Some Psychology on Inherited Money Mindsets

. . . .

Danielle R. Busby, Ph.D.

Licensed Clinical Psychologist & Co-founder of
Black Mental Wellness (www.blackmentalwellness.com)

S o, where do we even start? The information presented throughout this book can all find its way back to our human mind, our brain. Our human brain is complex—both biological and environmental factors can influence its physical structure and functioning. As a result, our brain directly impacts how we think, feel, and behave. The root of our inherited money mindsets links directly to our thoughts, feelings, and behaviors. Thoughts, feelings, and behaviors are the three primary components of one type of therapy called Cognitive Behavioral Therapy (CBT). This section will share how you can use CBT–based strategies to face and transform your inherited money mindsets.

So, What Do We Know?

When performing a therapeutic intervention assessment—essentially an opportunity to modify behavior— a few questions must be asked. What do we know? What do we do after we clearly identify what we know? What do we know about what we know?

In answering these questions, we can begin to identify CBT–based skills and strategies that you could apply when you engage behaviors rooted in stagnant money mindsets —especially those that negatively impact your financial health and legacy.

Fortunately, the research has already provided the answers to these questions for us.

Research Proves That Racism Exhausts Black Americans

Multiple studies have done an effective job documenting the truth that many of us already know and feel daily. Racism is exhausting!

Individual and systemic racism not only takes a toll on an array of financial outcomes for black Americans. Racism (in its many forms) also can negatively impact the physical, physiological, and psychological health of black Americans.

Specifically, both cumulative and chronic experiences of racial discrimination have been linked to elevated blood pressure (like we need any more help with that), increased heart rate, and cardiovascular disease risk. Further, empirical research has indicated that racial discrimination is associated with greater exhibited symptoms related to mental health conditions, including depression, suicidal risk, violence, stress disorders, and maladaptive coping methods (i.e., substance use).

So What?

This cumulative distress can affect your money mindsets and your money related decisions! Let me explain how. When we experience greater symptoms related to mental health outcomes or conditions, other areas related to decision making are impacted. Unfortunately, decisions related to money, such as how we spend our money, are not exempt from this impact. For example, if you are struggling with symptoms of depression, you may also be likely to struggle with your thoughts in other areas, like finances.

How Can We Overcome This Challenge with CBT?

Cognitive Behavioral Therapy or CBT is a therapeutic intervention often used by various mental health practitioners comprised of techniques specific to the relationship between thoughts, feelings, and behaviors. CBT is effective for motivated individuals who want a problem behavior to change quickly. Do you have any behavior related to inherited money mindsets that you would like to change?

If so, a primary component of CBT is Practice! **You must consistently practice strategies across situations.** The strategies listed below provide a brief overview of CBT strategies that you can implement specific to each inherited money mindset.

However, it is key to acknowledge the common barriers this particular strategy may impose. While implementing a strong set of techniques can affect change, it is key to note that many of the symptoms of common mental health conditions (i.e., depression, low motivation) can make implementing some example strategies more difficult. If you are concerned that may be the case for you or have additional questions, please consult a licensed professional regarding your use of CBT strategies and skills. It may be helpful to seek out a therapist with this specific theoretical orientation to learn more.

What can you do about inherited money mindset challenges?

Inherited Money Mindsets

- *Focusing on taking care of the generation before us instead of creating a financial legacy for generations that follow us.*

- *Giving when guilted and saving sporadically instead of giving impactfully, saving intentionally, and investing strategically.*

CBT Strategies

First, I want to begin by stating that the internal desire to want to take care of the people (i.e., parents, siblings, grandparents, close family and friends) who have helped take care of you makes sense. Internally, we want to care for those who consistently love and care for us. So, when it comes to this inherited money mindset, I think it is always important to begin by acknowledging and assessing where this internal desire comes from and to not place any value or judgment on yourself for having this internal desire.

Ask yourself, do I feel this is my responsibility?

Do I feel obligated?

Do I have a range of feelings that may even contradict each other?

Name them.

Accept the reality of them.

Become present to their existence and why they exist.

Engaging in this practice of self-monitoring and increased self-awareness is a basic CBT strategy that emphasizes that we must first become aware of the problem to address a problem. Keep a record of your thoughts.

When do thoughts related to this inherited mindset come up the most for you?

Is there a particular time of year (i.e., the holidays, birthdays, etc.) they feel most intense?

Is there a particular time of day they are more frequent?

Really clarifying what thoughts you are having and when they appear the most is an essential first step to addressing these inherited money mindsets. However, a clear next step to this acknowledgment and assessment is to help yourself intervene and respond. A common CBT strategy, cognitive restructuring, is a strategy used to help identify possible negative thoughts (or irrational thoughts) you may be having and work to modify them. For example, if I commonly think I am a "bad daughter" if I do not take care of the generation of people who took care of me. I would first need to identify that this is a common thought I experience. Then identify when I commonly experience it.

Next, I would engage in a thought replacement activity of reframing or restructuring that thought every time I have it. For example, I can think, "I am doing the best I can, with what I have to create financial wealth for myself and future generations." I could also think, "I am a good daughter for all the ways I support my family, including listening when they are having a difficult day, running an errand that they may need, etc." It is a common experience for individuals to stay in a negative or irrational thought cycle once it begins. However, we know that if we can intervene in our thoughts or our behaviors, we have a greater likelihood of shifting possible negative feelings associated with our thoughts and behaviors.

Additionally, it is so important to ask for support *and* "put on your own oxygen mask first." The thought patterns we are discussing are not always easy to identify by yourself. Seeking help from a professional provider is one source of help. Letting your close family and friends know that this is difficult for you and working to create the best balance can also help you keep yourself accountable.

Ask someone you trust about a common thought you are experiencing. I often think of including the support of trusted friends and family as a way to "check the facts" on the thought cycles we may be having.

Is it rational?

Are there appropriate boundaries or limits you could put in place to help with a particular recurrent thought cycle?

Are they grounded in truth?

Or are they distorted due to other emotions that may be influencing them?

All important questions to first ask yourself, and then ask close friends and family if you are struggling on your own. Further, the phrase "put your oxygen mask on first" is what we commonly hear when on an airplane and an analogy therapist use often. Essentially, if you are unable to set the appropriate limits and boundaries to make sure you are well, including your financial wellness, you will not be in the position to help others, including your family. Filling up your cup to pour and give (when truly ready) is necessary for maintaining wellness across time.

Inherited Money Mindsets

- *Buying an abundance of depreciating assets that deflate our financial portfolios versus intentionally gaining appreciating assets.*

CBT Strategies

One primary way to respond to these inherited money mindsets is to be incredibly clear regarding your goal setting and monitoring. Clear and measurable goals can help create purpose and direction and ultimately help motivate healthy financial behaviors. However, we also know that goals are often a source of stress for individuals dealing with a range of major stressors. Starting with one clear goal at a time can help assist with striking an appropriate balance. Making clear goals to identify both the long and short-term consequences of that goal is beneficial.

Assessing your goals and dealing with the best ways to engage in problem-solving when difficulties arise is another helpful strategy. For example, using the acronym SOLVED when working to engage in effective problem solving is a nice way to completely explore various possibilities. S stands for selecting the specific problem at hand. O, stands for opening your mind to every possible option available to you at that moment (even the ones you think are horrible options). L stands for listing both the pros and cons of each option visually. V stands for verifying the best option by circling your choice. E stands for enacting the solution, including the steps and time frame to enact these steps. D stands for deciding if the solution worked. If it did, great. If it did not, modify and rework your SOLVED strategy from the beginning to this same endpoint.

Intentionally setting up plans and strategies that make you give less effort to obtain a goal is helpful for some. For example, make saving automatic. Set up banking that allows you to withdraw funds automatically from your paycheck. Once paid, you can automatically place a percentage of funds in a separate account. This can allow an individual to spend less willpower on decisions related to saving or spending. For example, look for options that require you to wait a specific time period before you can withdraw the funds.

When you can, avoid the temptation to engage in spending. Instead of tagging along to the mall with friends, "to just look," is there an alternative social activity you all can engage in together after their trip to the mall? If you want to make sure you do not use your credit cards, leave them at home, and only carry the amount of cash you have budgeted to spend.

It is well established that an individual's money related thoughts, feelings, and behaviors have a significant impact on their overall wellness. So, take the time to examine your mindsets and, if needed, change them for the better. Find encouragement in James Baldwin's quote mentioned earlier in this book, "Not everything that is faced can be changed, **but nothing can be changed until it is faced.**" Face those inherited money mindsets. The work is worth it, and you are worth the work!

CHAPTER TWENTY-THREE

Your Legacy
Legacy Folder

> *Good people will have
> wealth to leave to their
> grandchildren . . .*
>
> *– Proverbs 13:22a (Good
> News Translation)*

Just think—through sound financial habits and healthy money mindsets, you could give your children and even your children's children a hand up from the financial pitfalls impeding the positive development of many black youth today. In a recent conversation, a friend posed the question, "**Could you imagine what our world would look like if every black youth that had a business idea had the capital to actually execute it?"**

What a world that would be! The great news is that you and I together have the power to shape and create a world where that is more often the reality. Investing can be a vehicle that assists our children and us in fulfilling our God-designed purpose and in funding causes that our hearts beat for.

Preparing for the next generation starts today and includes how we live our lives and prepare for our transition. Now, I can stand on rooftops and shout all day about how our community often does not proactively prepare for our departure from earth. I have *a lot* to say about legacy, so my next book with the anticipated title, "Our Children's Children," will delve deeper into this subject—Yahuah-willing. I plan to cover the topics of wills, trusts, and estate planning, tax strategies for legacy building, strategic leverage of insurance products, getting on the same financial page as your spouse, and more.

Right now, though, we are going to focus on one administrative action as it relates to legacy – which is to gather all relevant paperwork in one place.

Before we start, I want you to pause and dream for a moment. What positive experiences regarding money would you like your kids and grandchildren to have?

What financial legacy do you want your great–grandchildren to inherit from you?

Are you committed to doing what you can to see that this dream becomes their reality?

Your wealth is one key representation of the time and energy you poured on earth. Legacy is a gathering of the best resources you prized most to pass down to those you love. Whether it is financial, including houses and land, investment accounts, and trusts or sentimental like grandma's quilts, cookbooks from Auntie, Grandfather's carved dining table, or perhaps the Bible listing the marriage of your great–great–grandparents—you can leave a treasure trove to pass along as a celebration for a life well–lived. Your legacy bestows gifts beyond your lifespan to your loved ones. It illustrates generational blessing.

Now for this exercise, let's organize and identify your legacy items into a physical folder. You will likely want to also create an electronic folder stored in the cloud and grant access to your key legacy custodians. The goal here is to first ensure that you designate someone or somebodies (*yes, I said that*) who know where all of *your money 'tings'* are in case anything happens to you.

Second, you should gather all your physical and electronic financial resources and statements together so that *you and they will know* where the heck it all is. *I cannot overemphasize the importance of documenting your asset placement.* For instance, could you imagine having your random online savings account never touched or ever accessed again by your loved ones only because you never told anyone it was there? Let's not even add those types of problems to your life. Instead, let's pull together your legacy folder. You will find a checklist with all of the components you would need to put into your folder as an heirloom on the next page. Let's get to it!

Your Legacy
Legacy Folder

WILL /TRUSTS

Will? Y/N   If yes, what are the physical and electronic document locations?

Trust? Y/N   If yes, what are the physical and electronic document locations?

ADDITIONAL LEGAL DOCUMENTS

Do you have any other relevant legal documents (medical directives, power of attorney, etc.)? Y/N

If yes, what are the physical and electronic document locations?

LIFE INSURANCE

Provider _____   Policy Number _____

Policy Holder Name _____

User Name _____   Password _____

Physical Polcy Location _____

Value _____   Beneficiaries _____

LIFE INSURANCE

Provider   Policy Number

Policy Holder Name

User Name   Password

Physical Polcy Location

Value   Beneficiaries

LIFE INSURANCE

Provider   Policy Number

Policy Holder Name

User Name   Password

Physical Polcy Location

Value   Beneficiaries

LIFE INSURANCE

Provider   Policy Number

Policy Holder Name

User Name   Password

Physical Polcy Location

Value   Beneficiaries

ART

Artist

Appraised Value

Description

ART

Artist

Appraised Value

Description

ART

Artist

Appraised Value

Description

ART

Artist

Appraised Value

Description

REAL ESTATE

For real estate, let me give a couple of fictional examples:

EXAMPLE 1:

Name Smith-Lewis Family Home (Auntie's & Uncle's Home)

Property Address 333 Berry Lane, Jackson, MS 39211

Loan Holder – Yes or No. Yes. Auntie & Uncle pay me reduced rent to live in one of my properties.

If Yes, write the name of the Loan Holder. If No, write N/A. Merrifield Town Center Bank.

Location of Deed or Ownership Papers The bank has the deed. It is located at 1000 Prosperity Lane,

Jackson, MS 39211.

EXAMPLE 2:

Name Gigi's Family Home (Great-Grandma's Mary-Rose Lee Jefferson's Home)

Property Address 11117 Oak Street, Washington, DC 20007

Loan Holder – Yes or No. No. Grandma inherited it and gave the house to Dad. We manage it for him.

If Yes, write the name of the Loan Holder. If No, write N/A. N/A

Location of Deed or Ownership Papers We have a copy of the deed in two places. 1. A copy is at my house, 7773 Morton Lane, Fort Washington, MD 20744. 2. Another copy is in a safe deposit box at my bank—Maryland-Green Community Bank, located at 3000 Green Tree Drive, Suitland, MD 20746.

REAL ESTATE

Name

Property Address

Loan Holder - Yes or No

If yes, write the name of the Loan Holder

If No, write N/A

Location of Deed or Ownership Papers

REAL ESTATE

Name

Property Address

Loan Holder - Yes or No

If yes, write the name of the Loan Holder

If No, write N/A

Location of Deed or Ownership Papers

REAL ESTATE

Name

Property Address

Loan Holder - Yes or No

If yes, write the name of the Loan Holder

If No, write N/A

Location of Deed or Ownership Papers

CRYPTOCURRENCY

Platform

Username   Password

CRYPTOCURRENCY

Platform

Username   Password

OTHER ASSETS

ADDITIONAL ASSET

Description

Location or Access Instructions

ADDITIONAL ASSET

Description

Location or Access Instructions

So, What's Next?

First, I want to personally thank you for joining me on this path of creating a wealth blueprint for modern black Americans to follow! My greatest hope is that by picking up this resource, you see that whether it takes 2-, 5-, 10-, or 20- years or more—establishing a #7-Figure Net Worth is possible for you by establishing a plan aligning your habits and mindsets in pursuit of that goal.

Second, let's stay connected! I want to hear about your continued growth as you adapt and implement your own version of this blueprint. If you haven't already, please do the following:

 Join our #7-Figure Net Worth Facebook group.

 Stay connected for additional financial tips and insight by following me on Instagram @wisdomthenwealth. It would also mean the world to me if you tag me in a picture of you with the #7-Figure Net Worth book or wearing a #7-Figure Net Worth shirt.

Check out our website 7FigureNetWorth.com to subscribe to receive additional financial worksheets.

Third, has this book provided you with helpful insight regarding your finances?

If so, please share that fact with others by posting a positive review on Amazon. As an author, Amazon reviews are critical to helping get this message out.

Finally, continue to expand your financial knowledge and acumen. In addition to the texts that I previously mentioned, I also highly recommend the following books!

The Bible

———

The Wealth Choice: Success Secrets of Black Millionaires
Dennis Kimbro

———

Think and Grow Rich
Napoleon Hill

———

The 7 Habits of Highly Effective People
Stephen Covey

———

Total Money Makeover
Dave Ramsey

Also, 50+ references are listed in the Selected Bibliography, which I have provided for your review!

I hope and pray that many generations following you will be impacted because you read this book.

Believing that the best for us is yet to come!

Brielle Mabrey

Selected Bibliography

The bibliography is based upon reviewed materials for the following sections:

Your Numbers

Financial Assets

Fulda, Owen. 2019. "Sadio Mane spotted with cracked iPhone despite £150,000–a–week Liverpool contract." The Daily Star. https://www.dailystar.co.uk/sport/football/sadio-mane-spotted-broken-iphone-21179746.

Kurt, Daniel. 2020. "Emergency Fund." Investopedia. https://www.investopedia.com/terms/e/emergency_fund.asp.

Financial Liabilities and Debt

Bartlett, Robert, Adair Morse, Richard Stanton, and Nancy Wallace. 2019. Consumer-lending discrimination in the FinTech era. National Bureau of Economic Research.

federalreserve.gov. 2019. Report on the Economic Well-Being of US Households in 2018. Washington, DC: Board of Governors of the Federal Reserve System.

Kiel, Paul, and Annie Waldman. 2015. "The color of debt: How collection suits squeeze black neighborhoods." *Pro Publica* 8.

Mercado, D. 2020. "Here's why you shouldn't celebrate that big tax refund." CNBC https://www.cnbc.com/2020/03/06/heres-why-you-shouldnt-celebrate-that-big-tax-refund.html

newmiddleclass.org. 2018. "African American Financial Experience: Prime and Non-prime." Elevate Center for the New Middle Class https://www.newmiddleclass.org/wp-content/uploads/2019/12/African-American-financial-experience-Feb.-2018.pdf.

Nieves, Emanuel. 2019. "What We've Learned About Debt in Black Communities." Prosperity Now. https://prosperitynow.org/blog/what-weve-learned-about-debt-black-communities.

Seamster, Louise. 2019. "Black debt, white debt." *Contexts* 18 (1):30–35.

Personal Net Worth

Hill, Lauryn. 1997–1998. "Final Hour." Track 7 on The Miseducation of Lauryn Hill. Ruffhouse;   Columbia, 1998, Musical CD.

Belli, Gina. 2018. "The Surprisingly Low Salaries of Three Famous Billionaires." accessed September   12.   https://www.payscale.com/career-news/2018/06/the-surprisingly-low-salaries-of-three-famous-billionaires.

Household Income

Douglass, Frederick. 1995. "Chapter XI." In *Narrative of the Life of Frederick Douglas*, edited by Philip Smith. Mineola, NY: Dover Publications.

Insurance Coverage

Bieber, Christy. 2020. "HSA Benefits." The Motley Fool. https://www.fool.com/retirement/plans/hsa/benefits/.

bluecrossmn.com. 2020. "6 Benefits of choosing an HSA plan." Blue Cross and Blue Shield of Minnesota accessed August 29. https://www.bluecrossmn.com/shop-plans/individual-and-family-plans/6-benefits-choosing-hsa-plan.

Bradley-University. "How Mental Health Affects Physical Health." Bradley University, accessed August 29. https://onlinedegrees.bradley.edu/blog/how-mental-health-affects-physical-health.

Green, Nigel James. 2020. "The Deep Connection Between Your Health And Wealth." Forbes. https://www.forbes.com/sites/forbesfinancecouncil/2020/07/03/the-deep-connection-between-your-health-and-wealth/#ed70afb52aa2.

HealthCare.Gov. "Health Savings Account (HSA)." accessed August 29. https://www.healthcare.gov/glossary/health-savings-account-hsa/.

USA.gov. 2019. "Finding Health Insurance." USAGov, accessed August 29. https://www.usa.gov/finding-health-insurance.

Wiltshire, Jacqueline C, Keith Elder, Catarina Kiefe, and Jeroan J Allison. 2016. "Medical debt and related financial consequences among older African American and White adults." *American Journal of Public Health* 106 (6):1086–1091.

Credit Scores

Washington, Booker T. 2003. "Chapter 9." In *Up from slavery*. New York: Barnes and Noble. Original edition, 1901.

Your Habits

The Story of Shonna and Shawn

Agarwal, Kushal. 2019. "The Monte Carlo Simulation: Understanding the Basics." Investopedia, accessed September 12. https://www.investopedia.com/articles/investing/112514/monte-carlo-simulation-basics.asp.

Budgeting and Reconciling

Chang, J., 2020. *Americans Paid $34 Billion In Overdraft Fees Last Year. Here's How To Stop The Charges*, accessed November 12. https://www.forbes.com/sites/learnvest/2018/04/05/americans-paid-34-billion-in-overdraft-fees-last-year-heres-how-to-stop-the-charges/?sh=2a6492f03ce9.

Conroy, Brynne. 2019. "Budgeting With Google Sheets: 18 Simple, Effective Tips." Tiller Money, accessed September 6. https://www.tillerhq.com/budgeting-with-google-sheets-18-simple-yet-incredibly-effective-tips/.

Gorman, Ryan. 2015. "Regulators are going to start making banks refund your overdraft fees." Business Insider, accessed September 6. https://www.businessinsider.com/regulators-are-targeting-retail-banks-cash-cow-2015-4.

Merriam-Webster. "Reconciling." Merriam-Webster Thesaurus, accessed September 17. https://www.merriam-webster.com/thesaurus/reconciling.

RealMoneyTalk. 2018 "What Is Discretionary Income and How to Calculate Yours." Intuit Turbo. https://turbo.intuit.com/blog/real-money-talk/discretionary-income-1118/

Debt Reduction

MILWAUKEE. 2019 "US Adults Hold An Average Of $29,800 In Personal Debt Exclusive Of Mortgages." Northwestern Mutual. https://news.northwesternmutual.com/2019-09-17-U-S-Adults-Hold-An-Average-Of-29-800-In-Personal-Debt-Exclusive-Of-Mortgages.

Shain, Susan. 2020. "How to Find the Right Emergency Fund Formula For You." Chime. https://www.chime.com/blog/how-to-find-the-right-emergency-fund-formula-for-you/.

Warren, Andrew, Signe-Mary McKernan, and Andrew Warren. 2020. "Before COVID-19, 68 Million US Adults Had Debt in Collections. What Policies Could Help?". Urban Wire https://www.urban.org/urban-wire/covid-19-68-million-us-adults-had-debt-collections-what-policies-could-help.

Multiple Income Streams

Brown, S. Tia. 2017. "Direct Marketing Millionaire Breaks Down How it Works." EBONY. https://www.ebony.com/career-finance/direct-marketing-how-it-works/.

Collamer, Nancy. 2013. "Can You Really Make Money In Direct Sales?". Forbes. https://www.forbes.com/sites/nextavenue/2013/04/01/can-you-really-make-money-in-direct-sales/#1121b8a069c7

Stanley, Thomas J. 2001. *The Millionaire Mind*. Missouri: Andrews McMeel Publishing.

Impactful Giving

Covey, Stephen. 2004. *The 7 habits of highly effective people*. New York: Simon & Schuster.

Renting vs Buying

Avenancio-Le'on, Carlos and Troup Howard. The Assessment Gap:Racial Inequalities in Property Taxa-tion." Last modified February 2020. http://www.trouphoward.com/uploads/1/2/7/7/127764736/the_assessment_gap_-_racial_inequalities_in_property_taxation.pdf#page=55.

Clifford, Lee. 2020. "This is what every generation thinks of real estate—and what each has spent on it. "https://fortune.com/2020/07/17/generational-differences-real-estate-wealth-gen-z-millennials-gen-x-boomers-housing-market/.

The Hill, accessed September 12. https://thehill.com/homenews/state-watch/505648-newstudy-finds-systemic-racisms-in-property-tax-assessments-report.

Kapfidze, Tendayi. "LendingTree Analysis Reveals Mortgage Denials at Cycle Low." LendingTree.com. October 17, 2019. Accessed September 12, 2020. https://www.lendingtree.com/mortgage-denials-at-cycle-low/.

Leigh, Wilhelmina, and Danielle Huff. 2007. "African Americans and homeownership: separate and unequal, 1940 to 2006." Washington, DC: The Joint Center for Political Economic Studies.

Moreno, J. Edward. 2020. "New study finds systemic racism in property tax assessments: report."

Rothstein, Richard. 2017. "Preface." In The color of law: A forgotten history of how our government segregated America. New York: Liveright Publishing.

Intentional Savings

crfb.org. 2019. "Cory Booker's "Baby Bonds" Plan." Committee for a Responsible Federal Budget. http://www.crfb.org/blogs/cory-bookers-baby-bonds-plan.

Eum, Jennifer. 2014. "Want To Be A Millionaire In Retirement? Start Saving 10% Of Your Salary In Your 20s." Forbes. https://www.forbes.com/sites/jennifereum/2014/10/30/want-to-be-a-millionaire-in-retirement-start-saving-10-of-your-salary-in-your-20s/#18dc56b24444.

Gould, Elise. 2020. "Black-White Wage Gaps Are Worse Today than in 2000." *Working Economics*.

Reid, Pauleanna. 2020. "How To Close The Inequality Wealth Gap According To 5 Black Women In Finance." Forbes. https://www.forbes.com/sites/pauleannareid/2020/03/31/how-to-close-the-inequality-wealth-gap-according-to-5-black-women-in-finance/#12a1a7dc75b5.

Shapiro, Thomas, Tatjana Meschede, and Sam Osoro. 2013. "The roots of the widening racial wealth gap: Explaining the black-white economic divide. Institute on Assets and Social Policy." Institute on Assets & Social Policy-Brandeis University https://heller.brandeis.edu/iasp/pdfs/racial-wealth-equity/racial-wealth-gap/roots-widening-racial-wealth-gap.pdf.

Valentine, Debra A. 1998. "Pyramid Schemes - International Monetary Funds Seminar on Current Legal Issues Affecting Central Banks." Federal Trade Commission. https://www.ftc.gov/public-statements/1998/05/pyramid-schemes.

Assembling Your Financial Squad

Berry-Johnson, Janet. 2019. "The Big List of Small Business Tax Deductions (2020)." BENCH. https://bench.co/blog/tax-tips/small-business-tax-deductions/.

Nowacki, Lauren. 2019. "Financial Coach vs. Financial Advisor: What's the Difference?". Quicken Loans. https://www.quickenloans.com/blog/financial-coach-vs-financial-advisor.

Investing

Bambrough, Billy. 2020. "If Billionaire Investor Warren Buffett Ever Buys Bitcoin You Should Probably Sell." Forbes, accessed September 6. https://www.forbes.com/sites/billybambrough/2020/02/26/if-billionaire-investor-warren-buffett-ever-buys-bitcoin-you-should-probably-sell/#e770a591152c.

Corben, Billy. 2009. BROKE. In *30 for 30*: ESPN Films.

Desilver, Drew. 2013. "Black unemployment rate is consistently twice that of whites." *Pew Research Center* 21.

Du Bois, William Edward Burghardt. 2018. "The Talented Tenth." In *The Souls of Black Folk*. Penguin Books.

McIntosh, Kriston, Emily Moss, Ryan Nunn, and Jay Shambaugh. 2020. "Examining the Black-white wealth gap." The Brookings Institution. https://www.brookings.edu/blog/up-front/2020/02/27/examining-the-black-white-wealth-gap/.

Richardson, Gary. 2013. "Banking Panics of 1930-31." Federal Reserve Bank of Richmond, accessed September 5. https://www.federalreservehistory.org/essays/banking_panics_1930_31

Salisbury, Ian. 2019. "Warren Buffett Just Revealed What He Learned from His First Investment — At Age 11." Money, accessed September 5. https://money.com/warren-buffett-annual-letter.

Stanley, Thomas J. 2001. *The Millionaire Mind*. Missouri: Andrews McMeel Publishing.

Thangavelu, Poonkulali. 2020. "How Inflation Impacts Your Savings." Investopedia, accessed September 5. https://www.investopedia.com/articles/investing/090715/how-inflation-affects-your-cash-savings.asp.

Your Mindsets

Inherited Money Mindsets

Baldwin, James. "Quote by James Baldwin." GoodReads, accessed September 18. https://www.goodreads.

Extended Family Impact

Kross, Kris and Jermaine Dupri. 1992. Track #2 on Totally Krossed Out. Ruffhouse; Columbia, 1992, Musical CD.

D'Agata, John. 2016. "Walking." In The Making of the American Essay, 167–95. Minneapolis: Gray-wolf Press.

Evans, K., M. Holkar, and N. Murray. "Overstretched, overdrawn & underserved: Financial difficulty and mental health at work." London: Mental Health and Money Policy Institute (2017).

Solomon, Danyelle, and Jamal Hagler. 2016. "The Racial Wealth Gap as a Barrier to Middle-Class Security." Raising Wages Rebuilding Wealth:128.

Money and Mental Health

Evans, K., M. Holkar, and N. Murray. "Overstretched, overdrawn & underserved: Financial difficulty and mental health at work." London: Mental Health and Money Policy Institute (2017).

Made in the USA
Middletown, DE
17 March 2021